Planning Our Town

was written for the young citizens of tomorrow who will some day soon be the planners and builders of the world. The planning of cities and regions, the renewal of old towns, problems of water supply and air and water pollution, traffic and transportation unsnarling, and the best use of open space are all part of the wisdom which Mrs. Munzer imparts in this book. She emphasizes the fact that no community is "an iland unto itselfe," so that the young reader will always consider his town and city as part of the larger community of region, country, and finally, world.

PLANNING OUR TOWN

Planning Our Town

Martha E. Munzer

FOR THE CONSERVATION FOUNDATION

ILLUSTRATED WITH PHOTOGRAPHS

Alfred A. Knopf   *New York*

The author gratefully acknowledges permission to reprint the following:

The newspaper report of the Roosevelt, New Jersey incident from *Land, Wood and Water* by Senator Robert S. Kerr, Fleet Publishing Company, New York, 1960.

The doctor's story in the Donora incident from *Eleven Blue Men* by Berton Roueche, copyright 1950 by Berton Roueche, reprinted by permission of Little, Brown and Company, publishers. The article originally appeared in *The New Yorker*.

The words of Wheeling, West Virginia's Air Pollution Control engineer from Consumers Union Report, "The Polluted Air We Breathe," Consumers Union of U. S., Inc., a non-profit organization, Mount Vernon, New York.

Brief excerpts of magazine or newspaper interviews with E. Maxwell Fry, architect, Douglas Haskell, Editor of *Architectural Forum*, David E. Lilienthal, former chairman TVA, Ben W. Heineman, Chairman of Chicago and Northwestern Railway; and from the news columns of John Crosby of the New York *Herald Tribune*, and Brooks Atkinson of the New York *Times*.

L. C. Catalog card number: 64-21617

THIS IS A BORZOI BOOK, PUBLISHED BY ALFRED A. KNOPF, INC.

To my grandchildren —
who will be helping to shape
the towns of tomorrow.

Acknowledgements

The assistance of many gracious and generous people made possible the writing of this book.

In the fields of city planning and urban renewal, thanks are due to architect-planners Eugene Henry Klaber and Robert G. Weinberg, as well as to Edmund N. Bacon, Director of Philadelphia's Planning Commission, Alan H. Jepson, formerly of New Haven's Citizen Action Commission, and Leroy A. Riegel, Vice President of the Milwaukee Community Development Corporation.

For information and advice concerning problems of air and water pollution, thanks go to New York City's Department of Air Pollution Control and to staff members of the United States Public Health Service in Cincinnati and Washington, D.C.

William H. Whyte, of the American Conservation Association, gave useful advice on problems of open space. Claude W. Nash, of TVA, acted as host on a tour of its eastern section. Robert J. Gumbleton, teacher, recounted the tale of the Newton School Project. Professor Roscoe Eckelberry, of Ohio State University, gave invaluable assistance with the Muskingum Watershed story. Dr. Howard H. Vogel, Jr., of Argonne National Laboratories, did the same for the saga of Chicago's south side.

For initial help with the transportation chapter, thanks are extended to Henry Fagin, Professor of Planning at the University of Wisconsin. In the study of Boston's transportation system, appreciation goes to Robert C. Davidson, consultant to Boston's Planning Commission, and to Howard S. Lapin and Peter Stern of Arthur D. Little, Inc. of Cambridge, Mass.

After reading the manuscript, Mr. C. McKim Norton, President of Regional Plan Association, made a number of useful suggestions. Miss Sarah H. Smith, librarian of R. P. A., advised and assisted in assembling the Bibliography.

For painstaking reading and suggestions concerning the entire text, special thanks go to Dr. Ralph Conant of the Joint Center for Urban Studies of M.I.T. and Harvard University, and to Dr. Nancy Kent Ziebur, friend and former student, of Binghamton, New York.

A word of thanks to Mrs. Frances J. Anthes of Mamaroneck for her patient, efficient typing and retyping of the manuscript. And to colleagues of the Conservation Foundation goes gratitude for their ongoing assistance, encouragement, and faith.

If flaws still remain to mar this volume, the final responsibility must, of course, be mine.

MARTHA E. MUNZER

Contents

PLANNING OUR TOWN

1 / Introducing Our Town

Here you are, back home after your summer holiday in the "wilds." The cabin on the wooded slope at the water's edge was heaven after the many months of confined hustle and bustle.

You didn't mind the long trip to the country store to get the staples for a diet supplemented by wild berries fresh from the field and fish fresh from the creek. Perhaps you rather enjoyed pumping water for cooking and washing, and chopping wood for the fireplace and stove. Even the less agreeable chores of dumping ashes, disposing of tin cans, and cleaning kerosene lamps weren't really too burdensome — they belonged to vacation time. Everything was part of everything else and seemed appropriate to a scheme of things the family called "getting back to nature."

But at summer's end, isn't it rather pleasant to return to "civilization," to a home in which country chores are practically non-existent? Water at the turn of a tap in a tiled bathroom and modern kitchen. Electricity at the flick of a switch for unwavering light and for power to operate refrigerator, vacuum cleaner, radio, television, and countless other devices.

For a moment or two, contemporary conveniences, comforts, and gadgets seem miraculous, but they soon become the commonplace background of everyday life. And this change takes place whether the home to which you return is a modernized farmhouse, a suburban ranch house, or a city apartment house.

When you stop to think of it, your fundamental physical needs, aside from a roof over your head, are the same no matter where you live. Let's pause a moment to list the items which must somehow be supplied to you and your family, regardless of your surroundings.

First, there must be water for drinking, cooking, and washing, whether you dip it from a stream, pump it from a well, or get your supply by simply turning on a faucet. Equal in importance is food, no matter where you get it: from your own garden, at a roadside stand, or packaged and frozen at the supermarket.

Next, you require heat for the preparation of food — heat supplied by an open wood fire, a coal stove, an up-to-the-minute gas or electric range. And in all but tropical countries you need heat to keep yourself warm, whether that heat is furnished by pot-bellied stove, steam or hot water radiator, or by electric coils.

These are the important physical *inflows* of materials and energy needed by a single household, or a community of households, just to keep its members alive. In addition, no matter where you live, provision must be made to remove and dispose of the wastes of living: the garbage, refuse and ashes, the dirty water, and the sewage. These might be regarded as the basic *outflows*.

When you were roughing it at your summer cabin, your many chores kept you well aware of the sources and the destinations of the necessities for living. But back home, where life is so much easier, it is also easier to forget.

If you live in a large city, remembering is particularly difficult

The real heart of any large city is buried far below the ground. It is a tangled web of pipes, cables, and ducts.

due to the fact that many of the essentials of living are completely hidden from view. Imagine peering far below ground to the complex web of pipes, ducts, and cables, not to mention subways, buried under the streets of a city like New York. The tangle would at first seem like a plate full of spaghetti, as one underground workman described it. There are the gigantic tunnels or mains that carry a never-ending flow of clean water from the faraway mountains to the city. Buried pressure pumps send the liquid on its journey upward

through other, smaller tubes. Then there are tne sewer pipes and
mains that remove the city's liquid wastes. Gas pipes, many miles of
them, bring fuel to kitchen ranges. Still another series of tubes,
heavily insulated and reinforced by concrete, carry compressed live
steam from a central generating plant to tasks as varied as pressing
trousers and heating skyscrapers. Electricity is channeled through
hundreds of protected cables while a vast network of telephone wires
is housed in another complicated series of cables and ducts. This
extraordinary maze constitutes the root system that nourishes the
city.

But providing sturdy roots is only one part of developing and maintaining a healthy community. There are dozens of other requirements. To become more fully aware of these needs, we have only to
take a stroll through any community — your town, my town, or the
town the American playwright, Thornton Wilder, called "Our Town."

For our stroll I have chosen the village of Mamaroneck. One of
the reasons for this selection is that this community happens to be
"My Town." And besides, Mamaroneck is not too different from
other towns and villages bordering almost any of our American cities.

How can I give you the flavor of this particular town, this three-
century-old village forty-five minutes from the large metropolitan
center of New York? We might start at the old-fashioned and musty
railroad station whose only modern feature is its metered parking
area. From there we wander up Mamaroneck Avenue, a typical and
undistinguished Main Street except for the widely spaced trees that
add a note of grace. There are shops of every variety from the shoe-
maker's to the supermarket; from the inevitable five-and-ten to the
not-too-new, but nonetheless air-conditioned, movie theater; from
banks and hardware stores to apparel and novelty shops. Though
window displays are attractive, the store fronts themselves are a
hodgepodge of non-design. They are not dilapidated; it is simply
that small heed was paid to the beauty of the buildings in them-

selves or in relation to their neighbors. With a little more fore-thought, and at no greater expense, might not a far better looking shopping district have been created?

Though the village main street is pleasantly wide, we notice that car owners are short of parking spaces. And traffic gets snarled despite the overhead signal light and the busy policeman.

Mamaroneck Avenue ends abruptly at the point where it meets the Boston Post Road, famed for its history and its ceaseless flow of traffic. There are trucks that noisily move goods of all kinds into and out of the big metropolis to the south. There are occasional buses that carry workmen and shoppers to and fro between neighboring villages. There are private cars whose drivers are bent on such local errands as refueling their cars or themselves at one of the many service stations or eating places that line the busy thoroughfare.

To the southeast of the Post Road lies the area that gives greatest distinction to the village — the area that encompasses the beautiful coves and bays and inlets that make up the shoreline of Long Island Sound. Indians are believed to have wandered along the water's edge some five thousand years ago, fishing and hunting. It is thought that Indian families finally settled in the moist, cool region at about the time of the birth of Christ.

In the sixteen hundreds came the Dutch, and after them, the British. In 1661, the land that is now Mamaroneck was acquired by John Richbell, a native of Hampshire, England. Historians are not sure whether Mamaroneck took its name from a local Indian chief, or because the mouth of its small river, as recorded in old surveys, marks the place where, in Indian language, "fresh water falls into the salt at high water marke."

But to leave historical riddles aside, let's get on with our walk and cross the Boston Post Road. We find ourselves at Harbor Island — an island no longer, to be sure, but rather a filled-in expanse of open land for community recreation. To the right of the entrance is a high-towered red brick public building which bears no identifica-

tion. In Harbor Island proper there are playgrounds for young children, ball fields and tennis courts for teenagers and their elders. Best of all is the white curve of sandy beach, available throughout the year for the enjoyment of villagers of all ages and of all degrees of hardihood. Sailboats and launches lie at anchor in the harbor along with elaborate cabin cruisers and humble rowboats. On the pier, when swimming season is over, stand the patient fishermen, taking the sun and, ever hopefully, the catch of flounders and snappers.

For months there was a huge sign at the entrance to Harbor Island in plain sight of the Post Road. The sign read "Save Harbor Island for Our Children. Write or Wire the Governor." The billboard has come down, for Mamaroneck lost its fight to prevent an enlarged county sewage disposal plant from bordering its play area. Two other locations were considered for the dubious honor. No one wanted the new installation — but everyone needed it. Furthermore, there was already a small, inoffensive plant on county-owned land at the entrance to Harbor Island. The unmarked red brick structure we passed on our walk was the original building. And now that we have identified it, we can't help wondering why a sewage disposal plant was ever, in the first place, erected on property so ideally suited to the expanding recreational needs of the community.

Be that as it may, the ballots for the location of the enlarged plant were cast by the County's Board of Supervisors, and approved by referendum of the County's voters. Part of the land around Harbor Island is forever lost to children, but their lives and their children's lives in turn, are actually being saved — at a cost. Might some other spot have been found in open country where future play space wasn't so desirable and accessible? Was there indeed no suitable spot left, or was it primarily a question of dollars and cents?

A walk is no occasion for solving a problem as knotty as this

Mamaroneck, from the air, resembles any of the small towns bordering one of America's large, sprawling metropolises.

one, so we leave Harbor Island and wander over to Orienta Point, to the beautiful and expensive tree-shaded homes that border the rocky shore line. Some of the large estates have been divided, making way for new and smaller ones. One estate has been converted to a beach club, another is now the site of a religious school. All the properties are well cared for and distinctive. Except for a strip or two of marshy land, no shore line remains for development or for public use. Two generations ago, Mamaroneck children were free to roam the shore, to swim and go crabbing in many of the coves along Orienta Point. That day has long since departed.

Recrossing the Post Road to complete our circuit, we enter a section of far less pretentious but decidedly well-kept homes and gardens. Most of the houses are of the comfortable, old-fashioned, white clapboard variety. There are a few apartments of the garden type, and several of the high-rise. No apartment house, however — so says the village zoning ordinance — may rise higher than six stories.

On the corner of Palmer and Fenimore Avenues, a busy intersection in the residential area, stands a row of one-story shops: delicatessen, stationery, liquor, pharmacy, and hand laundry. A blot on the landscape to some, a boon to others, these "taxpayer" stores are typical of the haphazard growth of many of our old communities. In any case, this small, unattractive neighborhood shopping center represents a compromise between the privacy of a residential section and the convenience of the residents. Does this commercial oasis belong in this particular spot? If so, might there have been village rules or ordinances that would have insured a more attractive group of buildings? Are beauty and utility necessarily incompatible?

Within a few blocks of the area we've been traversing are the schools, the firehouse, the library, the post office, the health center, the telephone building, the village hall with its municipal offices, courthouse, and police headquarters. Then there are the Masonic Lodge, the American Legion Post, and a generous sprinkling of spired churches of many denominations. All of these buildings, and what goes on inside them, represent the way a typical American town conducts its community life.

As we approach the railroad station once more, we discover a small, old-time cemetery, whose faintly-marked graves gently remind us of the passing of the generations of Mamaroneck's settlers.

I wish our tour might end at the depot. Unfortunately, Mamaroneck, like most other towns, has another side of the tracks. Let's explore briefly this small section of filled-in marshland bordering the far side of the railroad, where a number of the town's disadvantaged minority groups live.

As we wander through the narrow streets, we discover a few factories and warehouses, some new, some old, for plastics, metal products, building materials, and plumbing supplies. These structures, important to Mamaroneck's economy, are scattered among small houses, some of which are pleasant and in good condition, others in need of repair or paint, a few in need of demolition. Presently we find ourselves back at the station, having completed this short loop of our circuit.

Were we to take the same tour ten years from now, what changes might there be? Would the traffic on Mamaroneck Avenue be worse than at present, the village play space smaller, the public shore front more inadequate, the deteriorating section more dilapidated than ever? Or might the traffic flow efficiently and smoothly around a revitalized central business district with, perhaps, a landscaped pedestrian shopping mall at its end? Might the small strip of beautiful marshy land along Guion Creek, at Shore Acres, the next point to Orienta, remain forever wild as a refuge for wildlife and a delight for new generations of villagers? Might "the other side of the tracks" section be an attractive place in which to live and to work, thanks to the separation of industries from homes by means of a modern industrial park and a refurbished residential area?

At this moment, the shape of Mamaroneck's future is being vigorously debated at one Village Board meeting after another. All interested groups and individuals are being given the chance to have their say. The debate centers around a Comprehensive Development Plan prepared for the village by professional planning consultants. The 150-page document contains what is called a Land Use Plan, showing the proposed ultimate uses of all public and private lands, and locating the major proposed public improvements. In addition, the report describes how these goals may be achieved, and the tools that will be needed for the task: zoning, programs for urban renewal, improvement of public structures and lands, and over-all financing.

Does the Plan truly reflect the hopes and desires of Mamaroneck's

This unplanned jumble of storefronts is typical of any small town.
Actually, this street is in Ann Arbor, Michigan.

citizens? Does it need modification? Will the Village Planning Commission finally adopt the revised Plan as official policy? Will the citizens give continuing support to the Plan if adopted, and see that it is kept up to date? The way Mamaroneck's citizens answer these questions will determine the way in which their village is to develop and grow in the years ahead. Similar questions — to plan or not to plan — apply to any of our villages, towns, or cities, no matter what their size or where they are.

You and I will be adding our voices to the debates and our influence or votes to the decisions that will determine the future of the particular town or city that is ours. Furthermore, we will find it necessary to look beyond the town to the region, and beyond the region to the nation, for they are all inseparably linked. We will need, finally, to circle the globe in thought, if we are in any way concerned with a better environment for *all* the world's people.

A better environment means a choosing between alternative courses of action. We will need to inform ourselves on many matters if these choices are to be enlightened ones. Suppose we start our investigations from scratch, and imagine that we can design and build a new town — Our Town — according to our heart's desire and from the ground up.

2 / Our Town—
Planning a New One

If you could plan a new town exactly as you would like it to be, how would you begin? To answer this question you would need to know clearly what it is you expect of your town.

First, you would want a pleasant home. Your choice might be a house with a small lawn — not too much grass to mow — and a back yard where you could play badminton or at least have room to practice your basketball shots. Your parents seem to want this kind of home, too. Your grandparents, on the other hand, do not need their house any more. They say the care and upkeep are too much for them. They prefer a garden apartment. Your newly married sister wants an apartment, too, but a small, two-and-a-half room one.

An ideal town, then, ought to provide a variety of living arrangements — large houses, small houses, row houses, garden apartments, perhaps even a few taller apartment houses — to meet the needs and tastes and pocketbooks of your family and many other families of different backgrounds and interests.

And you would most certainly want community play-space: for ball games, for tennis, for swimming. If you are fortunate, there might already be a lake or pond on the town site. If not, an artificial one might be created. You would also try to reserve picnic facilities and wooded areas for roaming and exploring.

Then, of course, you would have to provide the indispensable public buildings designed to keep the town going and to meet the needs and wishes of the townspeople. In addition, you would have to arrange for the inflow and outflow of goods and services without which your town could not survive. Shopping areas and parking facilities would have to be conveniently located.

You would want some appropriate industries somewhere in town or on its outskirts, to provide jobs and help pay taxes. Furthermore, your parents and the other adults of the community ought to have an easy and pleasant trip to work and back home again. You would therefore have to furnish good local and commuter transportation and a rapid, safe flow of traffic.

Finally, you would want to reserve space for additional growth, and you might even think it wise to set an outside limit to the size of your town, so that its facilities would always remain adequate and uncrowded.

With these, and other requirements of your own in mind, you might try out a few designs. First, place a large piece of paper on a table, and sketch or build up with some modeling material, the natural contours of this imaginary town. Include the woods and meadows, the hills and valleys, the lake or creek. Decide which of the natural features you want to reserve for parks, playgrounds, and forest land. Map out the areas that are most suited for living, for shopping and for the educational, cultural, religious, civic, and industrial pursuits of the townspeople. Now, from clay or cardboard fashion the needed buildings. Finally, add the connecting ribbons of road.

There are dozens of different arrangements you might devise for your table-top town. Which pattern makes the most sense? Which provides the best physical environment for good living?

When architects and planners design a new town, or on rare occasions a new city, they first look to the past to learn how human communities started and grew, how they flourished, how and why they declined. Through this study, planners hope to avoid the mistakes that have so often resulted in blight and decay. Before going on with your own model, you, too, might find it useful to take a brief backward glance.

Human communities have a history that reaches back into the very earliest records, when there were far, far fewer people on the face of the earth. From the cave to the hamlet, from the hamlet to the village, from the village to the city, each step has been an answer to the human need for a life closely linked with others.

Particular towns and cities came into being because they were natural focal points. Have you noticed how many of the world's largest cities rise at the heads of great harbors, on the banks of lakes and rivers, or in places where other means of transportation meet and cross?

Because location has been so crucial, some of today's cities cover the remains of far older ones. Not many years ago, wreckers were demolishing a Victorian shop building in the center of London. Suddenly, a laborer, digging in the foundation with his pickax, gave an exclamation of surprise. His fellow-workers crowded round as he pulled from a hole a handful of broken, brightly colored tiles. A few hours later, experts from the British Museum were removing the fragments as though they were precious jewels. Further excavations revealed that the workman had stumbled on a tiled villa built by the Romans when they invaded Great Britain nineteen centuries earlier. The remains of other buildings were soon unearthed, thus providing new evidence that the heart of today's London was also the heart of ancient Londinium. Modern Britons, some eight million in number, were carrying on activities not too different from those of the few thousand Romans who had built their city "in England's green and pleasant land," half a century after the birth of Christ.

And in the course of the centuries, more and more people crowded into London, particularly during the Industrial Revolution. Gradually, giant industries began eating into the countryside for coal, iron and clay, thus creating ugly factory towns and grimy slums in the cool, green valleys of former days.

There were people who protested. "Is this the price of progress? Is this the way things have to be?" These questions were boldly answered in a book which made its appearance in 1898. The volume, written by a man named Ebenezer Howard, was called *To-morrow: A Peaceful Path to Real Reform.* Howard's proposal was this: Let us build *new* towns instead of adding outgrowths to the old and already over-crowded ones. Let us bring the town to the country, and the country to the town by providing for industry and agriculture as well as for homes. Let us surround and protect our new town — our garden city — with a belt of green. But to do all this, the whole of the land must be in public ownership or held in trust for the community.

To start completely anew, to build on such a fresh design, seemed nothing but a visionary's dream. Nevertheless, in the early 1900's, Howard's vision took on reality with the formation of a corporation called First Garden City, Ltd. Land was purchased on the outskirts of London, and presently the town of Letchworth was planned and built, followed a few years later by the town of Welwyn. Both towns afforded light industry to their settlers. By the mid twentieth century there were some fifteen New Towns in Great Britain.

Ideas have a way of traveling, and it was not long after the creation of Welwyn that the Garden City idea was tried in America. One of the early examples is Radburn, New Jersey, built in the late 1920's, sixteen miles across the river from New York City.

One of the first problems the designers of Radburn tried to solve was how to create a safe environment against the hazards of the automobile. If you live in a town with its usual gridiron pattern of square or rectangular blocks, you know how many accidents occur at almost any street intersection, accidents caused by careless pedestrians or reckless drivers. Might there be some way of separating the walkers from the riders?

A way to do just this was devised half a century before the automobile took over from the horse. More than a hundred years ago, Frederick Law Olmsted and Calvert Vaux designed New York City's Central Park. They described their traffic flow plan as "a system of independent ways; first, for carriages; second, for horsemen; third, for footmen; and fourth, for common street traffic requiring to cross the Park." This is how Central Park's bridges and tunnels and the now familiar *transverse* roads from east to west came to be built.

In designing Radburn, Clarence Stein and Henry Wright, architects and planners, made use of the ideas of Olmsted and Vaux. First, they did away with the usual narrow rectangular street blocks and mapped out, in their stead, superblocks without through-traffic. Specialized roads were then built for one use only instead of for all uses. Walks and paths were routed at different places from service lanes, which in turn were separated from roads around the superblocks, main through-roads, and express highways connecting Radburn to other communities. Thus, there was complete separation of pedestrian and auto traffic.

In Radburn's first twenty years there were only two traffic fatalities and these were both on main highways, not lanes. This unusual safety record seems to be due in large part to the physical layout of the town.

If you try this traffic control plan on your table-top village, you will discover that to bring about such a separation of traffic you too will need to resort to bridges and tunnels, where walker's paths and other kinds of roads must cross each other. How many of these over-and-underpasses will you decide to construct? Certainly, cost would have to be one consideration in determining this question.

Safety assured, beauty would undoubtedly be another of the goals of your town. Of the beauties of Radburn, the most striking is the vista of seemingly endless park winding through and connecting several superblocks into a neighborhood unit. Grassy lawns with groups of trees are edged with paths designed for children on bicycles and scooters. Private gardens add splashes of vivid color. And then there are the "turned-around" houses, with living and sleeping rooms facing toward the gardens and parks while service rooms front the access roads.

Unfortunately, privately-financed Radburn was born just before the days of the Great Depression. Money ran out and the unfinished town failed in two of the objectives of a Garden City. First, there was never a complete belt of green to encircle and protect the town from the spreading sprawl around it. Second, there were no industries to supply steady work for the residents, who were thus forced to join the growing horde of commuters. Radburn in its entirety remained a dream.

But the garden city idea refused to die. A number of other privately-financed preplanned communities were initiated and completed. Presently, our government itself went into the business. This is how it happened: In 1933, ten million American workers were unemployed and many public works programs were undertaken to help meet the emergency. Among the projects was the construction of three Greenbelt Towns under the auspices of the Department of Agriculture's Resettlement Administration. The purposes were: to give useful work to men on unemployment relief, to provide low-rent housing in healthful surroundings (both physical and social) for families in the low-income bracket, and to demonstrate in practice the soundness of planning and operating towns according to certain garden city principles.

Greendale, Wisconsin, one of America's preplanned towns, emphasizes the small, safe streets and girdles of green.

So it was that the Greenbelt Towns came into existence: Greenbelt, Maryland, thirteen miles from the center of the nation's Capital; Greendale, Wisconsin, seven miles from the business center of Milwaukee; Greenhills, Ohio, five miles from Cincinnati.

The Greenbelt towns, though embodying most of the principles laid down by Howard, lacked a firm base of home industry. They were pleasant towns with their attractive homes and community buildings, their safe, special streets similar to those of Radburn, their girdles of green. They were towns designed to give people an opportunity to come into living contact with each other as they shared the task of building a common community life.

In 1952, the government decided to sell the Greenbelt towns but, again, the idea was not allowed to die. In the case of Greendale, for example, when it seemed as though private developers were going to acquire fragmented portions of the land, a business man from Milwaukee, Richard P. Herzfeld, became interested. He persuaded three other business men to help him organize the Milwaukee Community Development Corporation, or "MCDC" as it was subsequently initialed.

Greendale is now in process of becoming a complete community. There are garden apartments for people who do not want single family homes. Here older people, like your grandparents, find a special welcome in the heart of the community. Then there are larger properties approaching an acre per home, each adding materially to the tax base. And, just as you planned for your table-top town, other dwellings of many kinds and sizes are now serving a variety of families of differing tastes and incomes.

Finally, suitable industry is being brought to Greendale. The first to come was the Allis Chalmers Research and Development Laboratory. Other light industries are beginning to fill Greendale's Industrial Park. These industries share the cost of community housekeeping and provide work for some of the residents who no longer need to join the ranks of those who commute to their jobs.

Well-located community schools, clubs, park and recreational areas aplenty, home associations for sharing the responsibility of maintaining each neighborhood, shopping services that remain intimate and personal — all of these give Greendale an air of being a good place in which to live.

The Greenbelt towns are small in size and number, their future still uncertain, but their influence large. They demonstrate the advantages of planning a community from scratch rather than letting it grow like Topsy. They reveal the advantage of single ownership of the land, with freedom from competing and often conflicting real estate interests.

In post war years, there have been a number of interesting experiments in preplanned communities, though most of the earlier ones are not truly "whole" towns. They are essentially residential in nature and are often designed for families of similar economic and social levels. You yourself may live in such a community — Park Forest, south of Chicago, or one of the Levittowns, on Long Island or near Philadelphia. In such projects, the private developer or corporation plans the town in advance and assumes the responsibility — at least initially — for public buildings and facilities such as sewers, gas, and electricity.

In many sections of our country, from east to west, other types of development have come into being. Those that have offered variety in housing, and have successfully provided for and attracted industries, are becoming not only towns but even cities. You will find, for example, Port Charlotte on the coast of Florida, a city with a land

From the air, the residential community of Levittown, in New Jersey, seems laid out with geometric precision.

area larger than that of Detroit; El Dorado Hills, near Sacramento, California, a town designed for 60,000 people; Hawaii Kai in our 50th state, a city that may well become the second largest in Hawaii.

Within the last year or two there has been a new surge of interest in the original New Town idea. There are, at present, about twenty preplanned communities in the design or construction stage. It may well be that our country is on the verge of a New Town boom.

In Orange County, California, between Los Angeles and San Diego, there are master plans for converting a gigantic ranch, six times the size of Manhattan Island, into three complete communities. Peach Tree City near Atlanta, Georgia, Clear Lake City on ranchland near Houston, Texas, and Colorado City, just south of Pueblo, are other examples. These New Towns are also called *Satellite Cities*, a name which implies that they have close connections with a large nearby metropolis.

Balanced Community is another name, indicating that the New Town is provided with necessary services, facilities, and work opportunities, and in addition has made provision for a varied rather than a one-class population.

One of the New Towns generally considered to be outstanding in quality of planning and design is Reston, Virginia. Eighteen miles to the west of Washington, D.C., Reston is set in a region of wooded hillsides and gently sloping pastures. The design of the seven villages of ten thousand residents each will preserve and utilize the natural features of the land. Other features are being added as, for example, an artificial lake around which the first village is being built.

Today, American New Towns, unlike the British which are government planned, financed, and controlled, are a product of private enterprise. Should Congress pass legislation providing financial aid for community development on state, local, and developer levels, it may well be that we in the United States will be able to create balanced communities on a truly significant scale.

No story of preplanned communities, no matter how brief, would be complete without reference to the schematic plan for a city made by the famous American architect, Frank Lloyd Wright.

Wright believed that "when every man, woman, and child may be born to put his feet on his own acres and every unborn child finds his acre waiting for him when he is born — then democracy will have been realized." Wright's dream took shape in "Broadacre City."

One of the features of the plan for Broadacre City was that the buildings would all take on, in endless variety, the nature and char-

Reston, Virginia is still in the planning and building stages, but this lifelike model indicates its quality.

acter of the ground on which they stood, so that it would be difficult
to see where the ground left off and the building began. All buildings were to be integral parts — organic features — of the ground,
according to place and purpose.

Residents of Broadacre City would choose their work, their self-
improvement, their recreation, within a radius of ten to forty minutes
from their homes. All of these activities were to be available by
means of private car, plane, helicopter, or some other form of fast
public conveyance. Wright declared that "the means to live a more
lovable life now demands a more livable city." Broadacre was his
answer to "the grim boxing of families, tier on tier — row on row —
behind rows or beside rows of other families similarly boxed."

Though Wright's plan for his ideal "living city" never left the
model stage, his ideas have been used — and more often misused —
in the hundreds of commercial subdivisions of our sprawling sub-
urbias. And it is to Wright, and his prairie style of architecture, that
we owe the popular, spread out, single story ranchhouse that can be
seen throughout our country.

At the opposite pole from Wright stands the world renowned
architect and planner, Le Corbusier, born Charles-Edouard Jean-
neret, native of Switzerland, citizen of France. Corbu, as he is fre-
quently called, feels that the typical Garden City is a place of exile
and disillusionment. He visualizes in its stead the *vertical* "Radiant
City," with high rising sun-drenched towers set in a beautiful park.
This plan, Corbu believes, is perfectly adapted to restore man to his
natural surroundings and to his essential joys — sun, space, and
verdure.

Corbu had to start out with isolated, individual skyscrapers.
Using the tools of modern technology — notably steel and reinforced
concrete — he freed his buildings from their massive foundations resting on the ground. He built his structures on stilts. No longer was
there need for thick, weight-bearing walls pierced by small windows.
Instead, a building could be erected by using slender columns of

the new structural materials with flat slabs for floors and roof. The entire façade, covered with a glass skin and shielded by sunbreakers, could now be used for illuminating the interior. In addition, the roof slab was a potential garden site. Here Corbu planned parks, playgrounds, and plazas, with "hills" for children to climb and pools for them to splash about in. Many of these roof-top gardens, screened by parapets from all but the distant landscapes, are places of singular enchantment.

In 1922, Le Corbusier had exhibited in Paris his plan for a "Contemporary City" of three million inhabitants. His cross-shaped fifty to sixty story skyscrapers were placed far apart in expanses of greenery. These towers were to house the city's "brains" — its banking interests, its business and industrial affairs. Beyond the central ring came the civic and cultural center surrounded by belts of apartment houses, with a garden for every apartment. Factories and utilities were relegated to the outskirts. Sixteen feet above ground came a network of motorways and bridges with side-shoots to the entrance doors and autoports of buildings. One hundred percent of the ground was given over to the pedestrian.

Corbu's "Villa Contemporaine" like Wright's "Broadacre City" was never built. But in scattered cities throughout the world stand his gleaming public buildings, his chapels, his homes and apartments. In Marseilles, Berlin, Nantes, his glass towers provide thousands of families with sun-dappled homes in the sky. Unfortunately, as with Wright, Corbu's ideas have been vulgarized, his forms and spaces and proportions distorted in the monotonous high-rise housing developments to be seen in so many of our own big cities.

Though his Contemporary City and his later Radiant City never materialized as such, Le Corbusier at the age of 70 had the rare opportunity of planning from scratch a real city of 89,000 inhabitants, and of designing its center entirely by himself.

In the late 1950's, the site where the city of Chandigarh now stands was just a rural countryside with the curved lines of the Shiwalik

Hills in the near distance, the snow-covered Himalayas in the far background.

When India was partitioned, the old city of Lahore went to Pakistan. The Indian government asked Le Corbusier to build a whole new city to replace it. Previously, Albert Mayer and Matthew Novicki of the American firm of Mayer and Whittlesey, had suggested a Radburn-like plan for the new capital. Le Corbusier did not discard their central idea of neighborhood development, but used it in his own highly original manner.

After only a week at the site, Corbu was ready to start — with nothing more than a half dozen concrete mixers and one crane. The British architect, Maxwell Fry, who helped with the work, said, "We had twenty thousand women and children, oxen and donkeys by the thousand. We got the big concrete structures up with a mess of cockeyed scaffolding. We really built it like the Pyramids."

A few mistakes were inevitable, the chief one, perhaps, the lack of decent housing for the city's lowliest workers, its "pyramid" builders. For far too long, gleaming Chandigarh was encircled by the miserable hovels of a shantytown.

As for the plan of the city itself, in order to leave the ground level entirely to people on foot, Corbu sank the roads, as open-roofed tunnels, down into the plain. The spacious areas between buildings he punctuated with large, clear pools and great sculptured mounds.

The major buildings of Chandigarh, with their pillars and sunbreaks, their soaring archways and intertwining ramps, their surprise openings and exciting façades, have been likened to notes on a great musical score. To some, this strange symphony is strident and disturbing; to others it is breath-takingly beautiful.

Chandigarh is strikingly modern, but its women laborers still carry baskets of cement and earth in the ancient manner (above).

Back view of a row of apartments in Chandigarh shows the attractive modernity of this newest city in an old civilization (below).

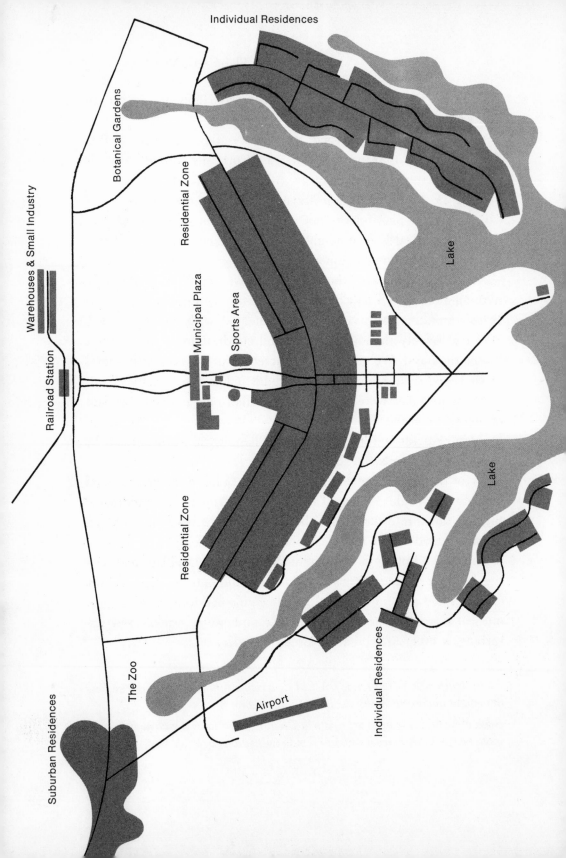

Individual Residences

Botanical Gardens

Residential Zone

Warehouses & Small Industry

Railroad Station

Municipal Plaza

Sports Area

Lake

Residential Zone

Lake

Suburban Residences

The Zoo

Airport

Individual Residences

The layout of Brasília, Brazil's new capital, closely resembles an airplane as befits a capital in the air age. Brasília is being carved out of the wilderness, a modern city growing up in the center of an undeveloped area.

In some ways even more remarkable than Chandigarh, and on the opposite side of the globe, stands another shining brand-new city — Brasília, the capital of Brazil. The city has literally been carved out of the wilderness. Choosing the undeveloped, fertile center of the country, the people of Brazil under the able leadership of their president, Juscelino Kubitschek, conceived, planned, and built, within a brief four years, the entire framework for a new kind of city for half a million people. The velocity with which this great city was built has never been equaled, at least in modern times. The sense of urgency was explained by Brasília's distinguished planner, Lúcio Costa, in these words, "We have to finish in five years or the forests will come back." President Kubitschek is no longer in office and the work on Brasília is still far from complete. At the moment it is partly a new and monumental city; partly a wooden-shacked, dirt-floored, rough-and-rowdy frontier town from which government workers flee during the long weekends.

It has been commonly believed that large regional cities must operate within zones established by close contact, namely by giving local farmers a market and local workers industrial jobs. Brasília, however, after a careful survey of the entire country, was placed next to nothing. Yet the city has already become a powerful stimulus for agriculture and industry miles away. This development has been made possible because roads and highways were planned and built along with the city. In other words, the new capital of Brazil is not designed to be a dot on a map but, rather, the center of a spider web spread over a vast, almost continental area. Modern transportation and communication have made possible this new kind of city.

People differ in their view of the architectural beauty of Brasília, but those who have seen it seem to be in agreement that Lúcio Costa, its planner, and Oscar Niemeyer, its architect, have created a vibrant city. When Douglas Haskell, editor of *Architectural Forum*, visited the city, he wrote, "Surely nowhere else has a monumental capital carried an air so generally innocent, lyrical, and dancelike."

But there are few places in the world — in fact only in the less developed countries — where the Brasílias or Chandigarhs can still be built from the ground up. In our own country, most of us live in urbanized areas that are already permanent features of the landscape. And to some of us, our old towns and cities and suburbs, despite their manifold problems, are the only places on earth we would want to live. So another problem must be investigated. It is not just a question of building a completely new and planned community. We must decide this: how can we breathe new life into our old towns and cities to keep them, in Wright's words, not only lovable but livable as well?

3 / Our Town–
Rebuilding an Old One

How an old American town is coming to grips with its problems, we glimpsed in our brief survey of Mamaroneck, New York. The process of planning such a town's future is a slow and laborious one, beset with difficulties. Yet Mamaroneck is a relatively small town. Its present population is about 18,000 and the Master Plan calls for 20,000 at most.

How much harder it must be to plan for the re-creation of our large cities with their hundreds of thousands and even, in some cases, millions of inhabitants. Yet most of us now live in cities or in their immediate environs. Even more of us are expected to flock to some urban community in the years ahead.

Why is the city such a magnet? First of all, it is the place where the most work is to be found and where jobs, unskilled as well as skilled, are offered in the greatest variety. Many, many people are drawn to the city in the hope of earning a living. Once there, some have little choice but to remain.

If you belong to the fortunate group with greater security and more freedom of choice, it may be that your family is among those who truly prefer city to country living. Working in mid-town, your parents often vehemently declare that they wouldn't dream of spending half their lives commuting, nor would they exchange what they call the privacy of the city for the forced good-fellowship of the suburbs. Then your whole family prizes the city for its close-packed variety, gaiety, and stimulation. You each have your fa-vorites — the Big League ball park, the museums and art galleries, the theaters and concert halls, the shops and exotic eating places.

Many of you, on the other hand, come from families who much prefer to live in the country — most probably the suburbs. If your parents are among this large group, they have in all likelihood sought and found a place where they can have a home of their own, and a patch of earth to go with it. They are also interested in sending their children to an uncrowded and, at the same time, first-rate pub-lic school. Though your family wouldn't dream of living in the me-tropolis, nevertheless, all of you look forward to visiting the Big City on special occasions for the enrichment, excitement, and fun it has to offer. You may especially enjoy its busy, colorful streets, crowded with all kinds of people rubbing shoulders in a good-natured hurly-burly.

But the hurly-burly, in most instances, has become too raucous, the confusion too great. Already crowded, most of our cities are bursting at the seams and are spilling out over the countryside.

How is it possible for such gigantic, sprawling metropolitan areas to solve their multiple and multiplying problems? Many cities, all over the country, are making the attempt.

Thomas Holme's map of Philadelphia in 1682 clearly shows the rectangular shape of the city and its quadrant divisions.

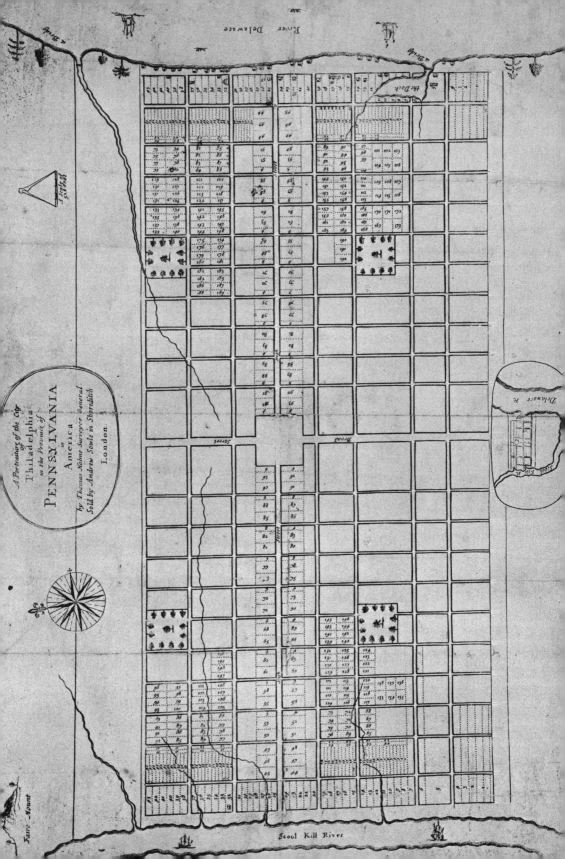

River Delaware

A Portraiture of the City of Philadelphia in the Province of PENNSYLVANIA in America by Thomas Holme Surveyor General. Sold by Andrew Sowle in Shoreditch. London.

the Dock

Delaware R.

Scool Kill R.

Faire Mount

Scool Kill River

One such city — our fourth largest in the 1960 census — is Philadelphia. Almost three hundred years ago, William Penn chose the tract of land between two northeastern rivers as the spot for his Quaker City, later to become capital of the thirteen colonies, and still later to be the temporary capital of the United States.

If you take a sheet of paper and draw on it a roughly rectangular shape, half as wide (north and south) as it is long, you have an approximate outline of the original city — two square miles in area, bounded on the east by the Delaware River and on the west by the Schuylkill. Now draw a line to bisect the tract from north to south. This is Broad Street. And the line bisecting the area from east to west is Market Street. Where the two intersect is Central Square, the site of today's City Hall. Penn's original plan for the city included four additional squares, one in each quadrant. These still form the basic structure of Philadelphia's downtown, giving the old city much of its charm and flavor. Penn's vision of the "City of Brotherly Love" was an open-spaced, well-shaded "greene countrie towne."

Moving forward in history, the bold planning of Fairmount Park, in the early eighteen hundreds, did much to preserve bands of living green for the growing city. And the city grew — not in any orderly way to be sure. It just grew, for Philadelphia had assumed the lead as a colonial and early American center for commerce, industry, and culture. Up to the mid-eighteenth century, it was the second largest city in the English-speaking world.

Philadelphia was a colorful place, with its shipyards, ropewalks, fleets of sailing vessels, and the displays of the handcrafted products of its well-to-do merchants. In addition, its solid-row red brick houses gave the city its own distinctive color.

Until the mid-nineteenth century, the metropolis was confined to its original rectangle, although suburbs were developing and were reaching far out into the open country. In 1854, these neighboring communities were united with the city. Today, Philadelphia covers an area of 134 square miles.

After the Civil War, a huge new terminal station was built to take care of the city's growing network of rails. If you look at your sketch, you can quickly select the one place where, from the future's point of view, a terminal ought *not* to have been erected. You are right if you choose the intersection of Broad and Market Streets — the very center of today's downtown. Nevertheless, the new station was built at Broad, and the open tracks and freight yards skirted Market Street. About forty years after the construction of this "Chinese Wall," as it was aptly called, the tracks were tunneled below ground and a new Thirtieth Street terminal erected. It took another twenty years for the "Wall" to be torn down.

During all this time, the period of steam and electricity, of concrete and steel, the city continued to swell. And at the same time, there were disturbing and growing signs of blight and decay. How did it happen?

In the early days of the city, its wealthy aristocrats built their homes in the most desirable locations. As time went on, expanding business and industry caused these founding families to move their large and elaborate households to greener areas. The original residents were replaced by smaller, middle-class families, who chose an urban environment because they liked what the city had to offer. But, gradually, the central city became too crowded for the newcomers, and they, too, moved uptown or to the inviting new suburbs. Over the years, more and more people of low income, generally minority groups, flocked to the city in search of a living. War and depression prevented new building. Housing became scarcer and scarcer. It was profitable to cut up homes and apartments into small kitchenette, share-the-bath units, and to convert fine old buildings into overcrowded rooming houses. Once-beautiful structures soon showed signs of age, neglect, and misuse. Decay and disease were well under way. The city began to die at its heart.

The story of Philadelphia's sickness is the story of New York's or New Haven's or Chicago's or your town's. For blight and decay have

inevitably followed on the heels of overcrowding and unplanned growth.

It was said by a wit that Philadelphia, the old town of William Penn and Ben Franklin, had degenerated from "the cradle of liberty" to "a hotbed of inertia." Those responsible for running the city, the incumbents of City Hall, seemed content to turn their backs on the plight of their town. But there were a number of civic leaders and ordinary citizens who were not content. They found each other and started to dream and to plan. Their *Better Philadelphia Exhibition* of 1947 created an image of what the city's future might be. Banding together for political action, the "Young Turks" finally succeeded, in the early fifties, in establishing a city government that was sound and energetic. Meanwhile, a new City Charter called for a comprehensive plan for Philadelphia. The preparation, adoption, periodic modification, and custody of the plan were put into the hands of a reconstructed and reactivated City Planning Commission, headed by an imaginative city planner, Robert B. Mitchell, who was succeeded in the early fifties by an equally creative planner, Edmund Bacon.

If you visit the Quaker City today, you will find ample evidence of dreams beginning to come true. The first is concerned with maintaining the eminence of Philadelphia as the vital center of a growing metropolitan area. The tearing down of the "Chinese Wall" cleared the ground for Penn Center with its tall new office buildings, its modern hotel, its lower concourse for shopping, its underground bus terminal, its parking facilities, and its tree-lined esplanades.

Then there is Independence Mall, planned as a fit setting for one of America's great historic shrines — Independence Hall and its surrounding time-honored buildings. The old sore spots of the neighbor-

The "Chinese Wall" in Philadelphia, with its open tracks and freight yards, (above) finally gave way to modern Penn Center (below).

hood — the defunct warehouses and factories, the flophouses, bars, and sagging businesses along skid row — were demolished to make way for a landscaped mall, and for the rebuilding of the entire section.

The second dream is less spectacular but even more challenging. It is concerned with the people's city and its rebuilding as a place in which to live and work. To build for the future as well as the present, to keep slums from breeding all over again, it is first of all necessary to provide the people of the city with an environment of beauty, safety, and convenience. Then — and this is quite as essential — the environment ought to give people a sense of belonging.

Philadelphia is attempting to satisfy this need for local identity by creating three kinds of units: *neighborhood, community,* and *district.* If you live in an already completed project, you attend elementary school in your *neighborhood.* Playgrounds and a recreation center are conveniently close at hand. You run errands to the small corner store only a block away. The high school, to which you travel a bit further, is located in your *community* which is made up of several neighborhoods. There you have access to a branch library, health clinic, and shopping facilities. To visit movies and theaters, to go on major shopping expeditions, you travel just a little further, to the center of your *district,* which serves five or six communities in addition to your own.

An example of this approach is Philadelphia's New Eastwick, one of the nation's largest urban renewal projects. It covers four square miles of low-lying land in a section that has always presented serious problems. A few years ago, much of the land was a mosquito-breeding swamp with periodic floods. Sewage-laden streams ran through the site; junkyards and shacks added touches of desolation.

Originally designed by architect Henry S. Churchill and today,

Defunct warehouses, factories, and sagging flophouses (above) were demolished in favor of a landscaped Independence Mall (below).

New Eastwick, one of the largest urban renewal projects, as it was originally — a desolate, shack-filled area.

under the guidance of Constantinos Doxiadis, well-known city planner from Athens, Greece, a development planned for a future population of sixty thousand has risen on the newly reclaimed land. You will find a community with a variety of detached, row, and twin houses, an industrial park with plenty of room for the large, one-story buildings required by assembly line manufacturing, a landscaped greenbelt, a linking system of pedestrian walkways, and overpasses reminiscent of the Radburn plan.

Not all sections of Philadelphia are in need of such drastic renewal as Eastwick. Wherever possible, fine old homes and other buildings are being conserved and restored, by private groups and organizations. Many individual homeowners, too, from a sense of pride in their newly spruced-up neighborhoods and from an awareness that improvements in their own homes will also increase the value of their property, have caught the renewal fever and are doing it themselves.

But what about the next generation? Will it, too, catch the fever? Imagine yourself a student in a Philadelphia school. You are going on a field trip to the Commercial Museum, where the Board of Public Education has assigned special teachers to conduct classes on a tour called "Panorama of Philadelphia." Revolving panels, lights, and sound track reveal and tell the dramatic story of your city— as it was, as it is, and as it hopes to be.

You also see exhibits of projects by various school groups: how the edges of a drab back yard may be transformed to borders of bloom; how the houses along a city street may be brightened with fresh paint and gaily-filled window boxes; how in a dozen other ways an old, dilapidated neighborhood may be transformed into a better one. You might become interested enough to get involved in some activity of your own, in your own back yard, on your own street, or in your larger neighborhood.

The question is: will this new understanding of, and response to, your city's still-to-be-solved problems stick with you and your thousands of classmates as you become adults? Only time will tell. And only time will tell what the future holds for such "brave new worlds" as are today being created all over the United States.

Unfortunately, the *new* has not always turned out to be the *better*. Thus, a number of the projects in our metropolitan areas have come under heavy fire. It is claimed, for example, that many structurally sound buildings have been needlessly demolished, that our cities instead of being rebuilt are being sacked. Others say that the high-rise, low-income public housing projects originally built have turned out to be breeders of new and more terrifying slums. Still others declare that not enough thought has been given to the displaced and relocated residents, many of whom may indeed be worse off than before.

There is a measure of truth in each of these criticisms, and we are beginning to learn from our mistakes. But, if we have any doubt about the *need* for community improvement, we have only to take a drive through the slums of any one of dozens of our cities or towns, large or small.

Having taken rather a long look at one particular city, and how it is attempting to solve its problems, let us glance at several others and single out some outstanding feature of each. First, we might visit New Haven, Connecticut, and pause at its famous Village Green. The Green was designed in 1638 when New Haven became the first town in the colonies to have a formal town plan. The original scheme, which can still be traced on a street map, was a simple grid composed of nine equal squares — the middle one reserved for worship and grazing. This Common of grass and elm trees became a model for numerous others in New England. Later settlers to the midwest carried the idea with them and created their own versions. Through the years, New Haven's Village Green, like those of its imitators, was the hub around which the city expanded, and the one stable spot in a changing neighborhood.

As the city grew shabbier and shabbier, there was mounting interest in the idea of planning for its orderly growth. A French-born engineer, Maurice Rotival, came to Yale University as Associate Professor of Planning in the year 1940. He believed that New Haven,

This is New Haven's Village Green circa 1890. The original Common was used for worship and the grazing of livestock.

noted for its history, its culture, and its bygone trade, could be made into a thriving trade and shipping center once more — provided its clogged and antiquated traffic system could be overhauled. This meant bringing more, rather than less, traffic to the city but allowing it to move freely. There were troublesome hurdles to be surmounted, among them the railroad tracks (reminiscent of Philadelphia's "Chinese Wall") which separated the Green from the once-famed harbor. Today, as part of New Haven's modern traffic system, the Green and harbor are reunited by a highway, which in turn connects with the parkway along the water front.

In the early forties, however, this and other parts of Rotival's comprehensive plan for New Haven were still on the drawing boards. There they remained for about another decade. Then, in 1954, a young man was elected Mayor of New Haven on the promise that he would bring city planning to life. Richard C. Lee knew how to dramatize the shame of his city. As an example, he publicized the disgraceful fact that ten thousand disease-carrying rats infested a single street in the center of town.

A capable administrator, Lee appointed able assistants, and, in addition, had the knack of getting people to work together and to accept good ideas, no matter what their origin. His advisory group, The Citizens Action Commission, soon grew to about 600 active participants. In no other city was there quite such a mobilization of community resources, all directed toward the creation of a brighter tomorrow for "Our Town."

Prior to Lee's election, urban renewal had received an enormous boost with the passage of the Federal Housing Act of 1949. This legislation provides funds for government purchase and clearing of old property. In the next stage, the government sells the cleared property to private developers at lower prices (sometimes much lower) than what it cost the government to buy and clear the land.

With the clearing of the slums near New Haven's Green, and the demolition of antiquated commercial structures adjacent to the

Green, a real estate man, Roger Stevens, decided to invest in this downtown area and rebuild the commercial site. He liked the City's political climate, its clean administration, and its good transportation. He was also inspired by the dynamic leadership of Mayor Richard C. Lee, the local initiative displayed by the City's residents as they worked with the City in restoring their neighborhoods, and the general enthusiasm for renewal that was in the New Haven air as exemplified by the Citizens Action Commission. With complete cooperation from City Hall, Stevens went to work, and today, stately old New England buildings on the Green's north side face the newly risen and gleaming façades — the hotel, office building, department stores — of the mid-twentieth century.

But we must leave New Haven and its rescued Village Green to visit another city. We reach the suburbs of Rochester, New York, on a cold, breezy morning. We race along on the superhighway into the heart of downtown. Not a single traffic light halts our progress to the 2,000-car garage, three stories below street level. Escalators whisk us upward.

Suddenly, as if by magic, we are transported from winter to summer. We find ourselves in the sun-filled plaza where children are playing around a fountain, gleefully sticking their hands into the spray. Mothers are resting on garden seats in the cool shadows of trees. Shoppers are taking time to relax at a sidewalk cafe.

Looking upward, we notice that the warm, sunlit mall is enclosed by a ceiling of mosaic glass. It seems that the entire area, the size of a football field, is completely conditioned against the vagaries of the weather. Strolling around the plaza, we pause to admire the displays behind shop windows and to glance at the modern glass-fronted office building with a restaurant and hotel on its top.

Facing the Village Green is a hodgepodge of storefronts (above). They will be modernized, as indicated in this rendering (below).

The sound of music attracts us to the center of the mall. Others are drawn in the same direction. There stands the Clock of the Nations, and as the hour strikes, animated dolls in gaily-colored costumes whirl through their national folk dance. When the hour strikes again, there will be other dancers of other nations.

How Rochester's new plaza came into existence is an intriguing story. It seems that Gilbert McCurdy and Fred Forman, heads of the two big department stores in Rochester's decaying central area, were worried about the flight of business to the smart new shopping centers of the suburbs. Ought they plan to take flight, too, and open suburban branch stores?

They consulted the bold planner and innovator, Victor Gruen, and his associates, who, after studying the situation, suggested an alter-

Midtown Plaza in Rochester, New York, boasts the Clock of the Nations. On the hour, the dolls dance to native music.

native to what seemed a risky branch store idea. There was further study and consultation with the City Administration; for without its consent and cooperation, Midtown Plaza could not have become a reality.

As a matter of fact, the city was already working on plans for the rehabilitation of its central core and the improvement of traffic flow. The administration agreed to close off a whole street, to shorten others, and to construct a huge underground garage, to make possible the erection of the Plaza.

Constructed in 1962, Midtown Plaza prospers as an ultra-modern shopping center with the festive flavor of an Old World market place. It is popular with the townspeople who arrange to meet under the Clock of the Nations. It would not be surprising, either, if Midtown Plaza were to cause a chain reaction in other sections of downtown, bringing new vitality into the whole city's life. The idea has, as a matter of fact, caught fire in a distant city. A news item in the fall of '62 was headed, "Rochester Has It, Boston Wants It!"

Rejuvenated central business districts are by no means confined to the eastern seaboard, but are being developed all over the United States. In 1950, to take one example, Denver, Colorado, was what a visitor described as "just an overgrown mining town." Ten years later, the redstone business core, reminiscent of the old frontier, had been replaced by a series of tall steel-and-glass skyscrapers, giving form to Denver's aspiration to be the Nation's Second Capital. The gleaming buildings of Mile High Center were designed in an unusual way, with a shopping concourse at basement level. The street level site for pedestrian promenading was made especially inviting with a fountain and pool to provide an accent of freshness in the heat of the day. Fountains have for centuries been used as elements of design. The shimmering spray, the movement and sound, are as welcome in an ultra-modern setting as in an age-old European square.

While these and many other efforts are being made to freshen and revitalize the hearts of our American cities, certain sections of industry are moving away from urban centers to find more elbow room in the countryside, or outer city. One of the finest examples is the General Motors Technical Center in Detroit, designed by the distinguished architect, Erno Saarinen and completed in 1954. Central to the design is an enormous rectangular lake, six feet deep and a little more than a third of a mile long. The research and development buildings are simple in design and carefully spaced around the lake. All distances within the site are scaled to the automobile and there is ample provision for parking on the sides of the buildings away from the water. The beauty and quality of this unusual center have had an important influence on later designs in other areas. The attractive industrial research campus is fast becoming a common sight as part of the landscape at the fringes of our cities.

We might, at this point, wander through any of a dozen urban centers such as Cincinnati, Cleveland, Pittsburgh, Providence, St. Louis, Sacramento — each in the forefront of planning, each with a distinctive and dramatic story of its own. Instead, let us choose another city and select an ordinary residential area which, we are told, has a far from ordinary history.

We enter a neighborhood of well-kept, old-fashioned homes and row houses on tree-lined streets. There are a number of modern apartments, open areas in process of being rebuilt, parks, playgrounds, shops, restaurants, old churches, new schools, a University campus, and a beach on a lake front; not a bad place in which to live and grow up.

Fifteen years ago, the Hyde Park and Kenwood areas of Chicago's south side were far from being good places either for living or for

Rejuvenated business centers are springing up throughout the United States. This is Denver's famous Mile High Center.

growing up. The story of the birth, growth, and decay of these sections, once the showplaces of the burgeoning city of Chicago, is the old, familiar one.

By the middle of last century, the first houses — seven in number — were built in the wilderness south of the city. Then one day, in 1855, a shrewd and ambitious young man, later known as the "Father of Hyde Park," made his appearance and bought three hundred acres of shore-front property. He arrived on the scene of his purchase in a new suit with $1.50 in his pocket and the rest of his capital in neatly printed cards bearing the inscription, "Paul Cornell — Attorney at Law." The young man made foresighted use of his property, immediately giving sixty acres to the Illinois Central Railroad for a right of way, on the understanding that the company build a station and lay tracks to take commuters to town and back. Elaborate homes with sweeping lawns and a magnificent, unspoiled shore front, soon made Hyde Park and Kenwood, its neighbor to the north, two of the most beautiful suburbs of Chicago. Over this domain Paul Cornell held sway as self-appointed supervisor in the early days when cow pastures still bordered estates, when water was sold by vendors at ten cents a barrel to those unlucky enough not to have wells, and when men still congregated around the wood stove of the general store to debate the vital issues of the day.

By 1889, the towns had grown to such proportions that they were annexed to the central city. Several years later, the University of Chicago, with its newly established campus, brought to Hyde Park a life of intellectual ferment and stimulation.

The next part of the story follows the old, dreary pattern — a gradual decline and overcrowding, the moving away of higher income families, more deterioration on the heels of war and depression, and the flight of middle-class residents as minority groups moved in. In this case, minority groups were largely Negroes from the virtual ghetto to the northwest of Kenwood. "For Sale" signs started to appear, as white residents, forgetful of the long history of their neighborhood's decline, blamed it all on their new dark neighbors.

The rest of the cycle seemed inevitable — the complete blight and decay of the community with no possible cure in sight except total demolition by the bulldozer. *But this did not happen.* And the reason was that the people of the community found voice and courage to say, "No, that's not the way it's going to be." From the University, from the Quaker meeting, from church and temple, from no group at all, neighbors met to see what might be done. There seemed to be three possible courses of action: They could pack up and leave the community. They could decide to do nothing because the problem was too big. They could go to work. They chose the third alternative. This meant a gigantic mobilization and organization of the community into action groups under the leadership of the newly formed Hyde Park-Kenwood Community Conference.

There were block meetings at which neighbors could thrash out the problems of their particular street. At one such meeting, held in 1950, discussion centered on the purchase of a building by Negroes and the swift reaction to that event. Four houses across the street had immediately been put on the market. "There are three alternatives before us" — so ran the discussion. "We could form a mob to try to drive the Negroes out. We could ignore them. We could visit them and ask them to join us in preventing the deterioration of our block." Again, the third alternative was chosen. The "For Sale" signs came down. Neighbors slowly began to regard each other with less hostility. Gradually, they started to join forces.

And the joining continued, as group after group — block committees, social and civic organizations, city, state, and federal agencies — became involved. Violators of existing housing codes and new ordinances were brought before the courts and eventually fined and made to conform. Block by block, the slow, tedious work of rehabilitation went on. Area by area, the process of decay was reversed. Physical planning, once discussed as an unpopular ivory

tower idea, was finally accepted as an essential factor in the community's regeneration and well-being.

The story of the rebirth of Chicago's Hyde Park-Kenwood Neighborhood is an unfinished one. Its outcome is still uncertain. Will neighbors continue to get along? Will blight be permanently halted? Will the community keep on planning for its tomorrow? The last question is the same as the one we asked in regard to Mamaroneck's future and Philadelphia's. We might ask it in respect to thousands of towns and cities throughout the world, whose stories are gradually unfolding. The answer — what happens next — depends on what choices, you and I and the rest, determine to make.

Aside from planning and developing good neighborhoods there are other decisions that need to be made. One of these affects the most crucial issue of all — the physical survival of the community itself. There are certain resources without which no community can exist. First and foremost comes water. In the past, we have too often taken an adequate supply for granted. This we can no longer do. Unless we make some sensible decisions about water, the future of "Our Town" may already be a thing of the past.

Before (above) and after (below) rehabilitation of a single home shows the Hyde Park-Kenwood approach to the problem of urban renewal.

4 / At the Turn of a Tap

A drink that looks like an ice cream soda — straight from the kitchen tap! Has it happened in your house as it has in so many others? Unfortunately, the froth always turns out to taste unpleasantly of lather. The explanation is simple but the solution far from easy. Household detergent has come foaming from the spigot in defiance of all attempts at water purification. This is only one of the headaches that confronts the sanitary engineers and scientists responsible for delivering clean water to our taps.

In the last two decades, more than half a million brand-new chemical compounds have come into existence. The residues from almost all of these substances are eventually carried away by streams and rivers. Some of the compounds have defied all treatment and have turned up intact many miles from the places where they were originally flushed away. And we are not yet fully aware of the dangers to health that lurk in these new industrial wastes.

A quarter century ago, you could travel anywhere in our country, turn on the faucet, and drink a glass of water without worry. True, the liquid might be discolored or have an odor, but you knew you were safe from the scourge of typhoid fever or cholera or water-borne dysentery. Doctors rarely treated people for these diseases, for scientific water treatment — filtration, aeration, chlorination — had virtually wiped them out. Today, doctors have patients with another illness that has been found, in at least some instances, to be water-borne. The infection is hepatitis, serious inflammation of the liver. In 1961, a record-breaking 73,000 cases were reported. Oysters and clams taken from beds in several coastal estuaries were

Too many of America's rivers — such as Lynchburg, Virginia's James River — are being poisoned by industrial pollutants.

found to be responsible in many of the cases.

It is not always a simple matter to identify the culprit causing a water-borne illness. The mystery pollutant that plagued an industrial town in Alabama several years ago is a case in point.

After the opening of a new bleachery, the residents of the town began to complain of the taste and odor of their water supply. Doctors noted an unusual number of patients suffering from nausea and digestive disorders. Sanitary engineers immediately inspected the bleachery and found its waste disposal satisfactory. Next, they went to the textile mill and it, too, got a clean bill of health. The pesticide plant, also, was careful of its disposal problem. Health officers felt that the practices of all three industries were entirely safe.

It was finally discovered that the harmful pollutant was being produced by a *combination* of the wastes of the three plants. Once the cause was discovered, the industries made the necessary changes in their disposal practices, and the water in the town is now reported palatable and apparently safe.

We need to add the word "apparently" to safe when describing today's water supplies, for we are still unsure of the long range harm done us by the growing list of unwelcome industrial additions to our waterways. Nor do we know the full effects of the insecticides and herbicides washed from the soil into our streams. Then, add radioactive fallout to the list of potentially dangerous pollutants. We are still far from knowing the full extent of the harm that may be done to the living things in the water by the accumulating poisons. But we do know that, in 1962, fifteen million fish floated dead to the surface of our American streams.

Before the invention of suitable instruments, the coal miner took with him into the mine a small bird whose sacrificed life served as warning of the presence of poisonous gas. Fish and wildlife play for us the role of the miner's canary. If our waters become so polluted that these fellow creatures cannot survive, it is indeed a grim warning to us.

Dead fish, belly up, signal a grim warning. It is a costly, tragic way of discovering thermal or industrial pollution.

Aside from germs and chemicals and unidentified "gunk," there is another form of pollution of which we are becoming increasingly aware. The growing industries in or near our towns and cities are using more and more water for cooling purposes. When this water is returned, it warms our waterways. A side effect of this rise in temperature is the lowering of the oxygen content of the water, for a warm liquid cannot hold as much gas in solution as can a cold. You notice this phenomenon every time a glass of ice water remains standing in a warm room. The small bubbles of air that can no longer remain in solution appear as tiny beads on the surface of the glass.

A river's temperature and oxygen content have a marked effect on the living things within its borders. Since our most desirable fish are found in clear, cold streams and lakes, trout, salmon, whitefish, and fresh-water herring are having a hard time surviving. A rise of only two or three degrees in temperature is sometimes sufficient to eliminate trout altogether. The water may become so warm that even desirable warm water species — crappies and sunfish and certain kinds of bass — are affected. The net result is likely to be that the undesirable species, such as carp, dogfish, and suckers, being more tolerant of heat and low oxygen concentration, crowd out the game fish.

Thermal pollution of water, with its attendant damage to certain forms of aquatic life, is not solely caused by the dumping of warm water into our streams. The cutting down of forests and their replacement with cultivated fields or with ribbons of asphalt means that the cooling shade is removed and the temperature of the water must consequently rise.

The denuding of our forests — a process that has been going on since the early settlers started clearing the land — has also brought in its train increased washing away of soil by rain and flood. The soil eventually ends up in our lakes and rivers, adding still another impurity in the form of silt or sediment.

If you have the opportunity, dip a glass of water from a nearby stream and observe the clarity of the liquid. Then you might let the glass stand overnight and see whether any solid has settled to the bottom. A bit of mud in a tumbler is a problem for you when you take a drink. Multiplied many million-fold, this mud causes what is known as *siltation*, with its attendant problems of clogged river beds and sediment-filled reservoirs.

For some forms of pollution man is not responsible. There is always a certain amount of natural erosion depositing soil and minerals into our rivers and streams. Then, too, some rivers are naturally salty. Down in the Southwest, for example, sanitary engineers are

When the forests are denuded, soil is washed away. That soil ends up clogging reservoirs and filling river beds.

working on a program to get the salt (or as much of it is possible) out of the Arkansas and Red Rivers. Oil field operations are responsible for only part of the brine. Engineers have painstakingly tracked down about a dozen contributing salt springs and beds. Now the job is to cap the springs or otherwise stop their flow. If this can be done, it will keep an astonishing 10,000 tons of salt per day out of these important rivers.

Sewage, industrial and agricultural wastes, radioactivity, heat, sediment, natural minerals leached from the earth — once you've begun enumerating the impurities that must be removed or rendered harmless before you turn on the tap, you become aware that you can no longer take a clear, healthful drink of water for granted. It is no simple matter to furnish Our Town or any other town with this prime necessity.

To help us in the task, we can count on flowing water's remarkable capacity to cleanse itself — at least up to a certain point. A stream's

Severe erosion on a steep slope will eventually lead to siltation. Trees and shrubs should be planted on the slope.

natural purifying agents are worms, snails, bacteria, and algae. Worms and snails dispose of the solids that sink to the bottom; oxygen-needing (aerobic) bacteria attack the dissolved and suspended materials; algae, under stimulus of sunshine, produce surprising amounts of the necessary oxygen.

A river system can carry off and render non-toxic, by its built-in sewage disposal system, considerable quantities of waste materials when they are sufficiently scattered. But when pollution is too heavy, a stream's power of self-renewal is not enough. Man must lend a hand.

The best way to lend a hand is to stop at its source as much pollution as possible. This may be done by various special kinds of treatment. But inescapably, we will continue to need flowing water for the removal of wastes, even after they have been treated.

If your town is a small one, solving the disposal problem may not be quite so difficult or so expensive as it was for many years believed to be. A chance discovery led to a new and simple method. This is what happened: In 1928, in the town of Fessenden, North Dakota, a new sewer system was installed. Because insufficient money was raised for the building of a mechanized sewage treatment plant, the town was forced to dump its waste into a hastily-dug basin at the town's edge. To the surprise of officials and inspectors a few months later, the sewage had somehow achieved a high degree of purification all by itself. No one outside Fessenden paid much attention. The pond was considered a freak. But it kept operating successfully. Finally, twenty years later, the town of Maddock, North Dakota, decided to install a similar pond. It, too, functioned well. Within three years, six other towns in North Dakota followed suit.

The U. S. Public Health Service then made a careful study of the basins and from that time on, the pond movement began to gain momentum on a national scale.

In 1956, a fifteen-acre lagoon in the town of Fayette, Missouri was officially selected by the Public Health Service as this country's first experimental station. A five year study was at once initiated. Officials and technicians from many other localities have journeyed to Fayette to take a long hard look at the pond which, throughout the years, has remained odorless and clear blue-green, and has provided a healthful home for turtles, and a refuge for loons and geese. No chemicals or mechanical means have been used to purify the sewage; the job has been done by settling and by the living things in the water itself.

Most public health officials now agree that sewage ponds are appropriate for small town use, provided the town has an adequate sewer system. For large towns and for cities, sewage treatment plants must usually be erected.

In a mechanized plant, as in a pond, tiny microorganisms are the agents responsible for the conversion of wastes into harmless sludge and safe water. The sludge is sometimes dried, packaged, and sold as fertilizer. Excess sludge, in its watery state, may even be burned up or oxidized in a process that uses no flame for the burning.

Sewage treatment plants are costly — running into the millions. But for many of our large metropolitan areas, and for some of our smaller ones, there is at present no other safe way. The need for treatment is so urgent that Federal Aid is now available to help municipalities defray the costs.

Although a number of towns and cities have installed satisfactory systems, the U. S. Public Health Service estimated that in 1962 more than five thousand communities needed new, enlarged, or improved sewage treatment facilities.

How does *your* town handle its wastes? Has it a truly adequate system for now and for the years ahead? How clean is your town's water when you receive it from upstream? How heavily is it chlorinated? How clean is this same water when it flows down to the next village? And the next?

Sanitary land-fill is one method of garbage disposal. The refuse is spread, compacted, and then covered with a layer of earth.

Once an efficient water treatment system is in operation, you might suppose that a town could relax. Unfortunately, this is not the case. Treatment does not insure anything but a supposedly *safe* water supply. An *adequate* water supply, plentiful enough to meet a town's constant and growing needs, is another story.

To see what happens when the water stops flowing, let us visit the village of Roosevelt, New Jersey. It is a place proud of its origin and development. During the days of the great depression, a completely new town was created with the help of the Federal Government. Unionized garment workers from the tenements and sweat shops of New York City came to Roosevelt to start a new life. Neat homes, gay gardens and vegetable patches, a fine school, factories in open surroundings, literally spelled a "New Deal" for the garment workers and their families.

The town's water supply came from an artesian well driven four hundred feet down to tap the underground flow. The supply was abundant.

Then one November morning in 1949, a sleepy official went to the tap to wash his face. He came awake with a start. A slight trickle — a gasping sound — and then a single drop or two. When he ran out to inspect the well, he found that the pump no longer breathed easily. It was spitting and sputtering and sucking up air rather than pumping water.

After an emergency session of the town council, the volunteer fire department drove its 1500-gallon-capacity pumper over to a neighboring town, got water, and set up a rationing system. The women, bundled up for protection against the biting autumn winds, stood in line with pots and pans for their daily share of the precious liquid. The water to be used for drinking was subsequently boiled, to be sure it was safe.

The garment factories had to close. The children, released from school, gleefully followed the water truck from station to station, shouting and joking. For the children it was a lark; they did not realize the seriousness of the situation.

A housewife described her life to a New York reporter: "My day is completely different now. We flush the toilet with a pan of water, and only when absolutely necessary. We drink almost no water but save it for our coffee. I don't bathe our three-year-old but sponge her with either baby oil or alcohol. We use paper cups and cook the vegetables in the can to save dish washing, and we stir everything with one spoon. We're going to a friend's house in a neighboring town tonight because they told us we could use their shower."

This particular story has a happy ending. The well had not permanently run dry for the citizens of Roosevelt. The failure was a mechanical one and life was restored to normal in three days. A new well solved the problem of a secondary means of supply. But will this prove sufficient in the long run? Will the town eventually have to find new water sources? The memory of those three days is still fresh in the townspeople's minds, and should serve as a warning to all of us as to the necessity of an adequate water supply.

The eastern seaboard is blessed with an abundant rainfall. But in the early 1960's came seasons of extraordinary drought. The summer of '63 was a particularly dry one, the fall even drier in the usually moist and fruitful region.

In Buck's County, Pennsylvania, the drought was so severe that in one section, all the wells ran dry. Neighbors from both sides of the Delaware River were reduced to drawing and hauling water from a single "gusher" that had been discovered when a local movie theater drilled a well for its air-conditioning system. Lawns, gardens, and vegetable patches had to be abandoned and allowed to turn sear and brown before the summer had even started. Water, suddenly priceless, had to be reserved for the barest necessities.

The residents of semi-rural Buck's County knew about the drought at first hand long before the people of New York City were shocked into awareness. Their jolt came in October, 1963, when the skies around New York had been cloudless for a record-breaking twenty-four consecutive days. Headlines told the story of reservoirs down to less than one third of capacity. The city had prided itself on its superabundant water supply, but the Mayor and his Water Supply Commissioner found it necessary, as a safeguard against future drought, to urge the residents of the city to cut their water consumption by twenty-five percent. Suggestions included the repair of leaky faucets; the use of pans instead of running water for dishwashing, shaving, and warming the baby's bottle; and the cooling of water in refrigerators instead of letting it run cold. The need for these and other homespun methods of water conservation point to the fact that a never-failing water supply can no longer be taken as a matter of course, regardless of past performances.

Other towns and cities across the nation, particularly those situated in the naturally dry West and Southwest, have, of necessity, been water-conscious from the beginning.

When the pueblo of Los Angeles was established in 1781, the Spanish Crown granted it the perpetual right to all the water in the Los Angeles River. Crude dams, water wheels, and zanjas, or ditches, distributed the water to the community. When the pueblo was incorporated as a city in 1850, a census accounted for 1610 inhabitants.

Though the gold rush of '49 passed Los Angeles by, the prosperity brought by the discovery of metallic nuggets in the north soon spread southward. Wave after wave of settlers flooded into the region and the boomtown at its center continued to grow until Los Angeles entered the ranks of the world's greatest cities. In 1963, it was second largest in the United States. Long before that time, the citizens of the city had to seek new and larger supplies of water.

Shortly after the turn of the century, William Mulholland, chief engineer of the city Water Department, dreamed a bold new dream. While prospecting for water in the mountain region far to the east, he came upon a large and crystal-clear lake. Why not tap this pure water and conduct it to his parched city? Mulholland's dream became reality when the citizens of Los Angeles raised the money by bond issue to purchase Owens Valley land and water rights and to bring the water 250 miles to the coast. The gigantic task of building the longest municipal aqueduct the world had ever known was started in 1907 and completed six years later.

Water from the snow-capped High Sierras flowed into the city, quenching its thirst and creating power needed for further growth. But as the city kept growing, the water began to dwindle. When Mulholland first glimpsed it, Owens Lake was a vast stretch of shimmering blue, nourishing the entire valley. Though water from the Owens region is still an important source of supply for the residents of Los Angeles, pictures of the area around the lake reveal a parched alkaline waste, drained dry by the insatiable thirst of an ever-growing metropolis.

In the 1920's, Los Angeles was again on its water hunt. The search led to the Colorado River, a river that was 340 miles away. The city, along with twelve neighboring communities, voted the two hundred and fifty million dollar bond issue needed to build the Colorado River Aqueduct, a mighty and ingenious engineering feat. The first water from this far distant source was delivered to Los Angeles in 1941. To reach southern California, the water had first to be carried by tunnel through six mountain ranges. At the same time, energy from the mighty generators of the Hoover Dam, at Colorado's Boulder Canyon, was sent by transmission line across 266 miles of mountain and desert.

For the moment, southern California was relaxed. But its new and abundant water source, the Colorado River, flowed with its tributaries through other water-short states — Wyoming, Colorado, New Mexico, Utah, Arizona, and Nevada. What right had Los Angeles and its neighboring cities to pre-empt this common supply? The question, brought up by Arizona, finally came to the Supreme Court and

and on June 3, 1963, the verdict went against California. The ruling stated that the tributaries of the Colorado are to remain for exclusive use of the individual states through which these tributaries flow. The effect of this decision is that Arizona is entitled to some of the water that California has been getting.

California, however, had not waited for the Court's decision but had explored other water source possibilities. In 1960, the voters of the state authorized the issuance of bonds totaling one billion, seven hundred and fifty million dollars for constructing the largest system of water conservation and distribution the world has ever seen. It will take over twenty years for the plan to reach completion. This means that by 1982, if no unforeseen obstacles arise, abundant water from northern California will be flowing through rivers and tunnels, lakes, and reservoirs from Feather River to San Diego County. During its seven hundred and forty mile journey, the water will nourish the land, serve industries, and take care of the needs of countless communities.

Meanwhile, Los Angeles has taken a new look at the Owens River Valley watershed and has embarked on a costly five-year project to utilize completely the water still available from that region.

But more water, accompanied by more power, further stimulates the growth of business and industry. This means more new jobs and hence more people. More people create new water needs and the spiral winds relentlessly upward.

Let's pause for a moment to see what are the actual water requirements of a single individual caught on the spiral. If such a person lives in a house without running water, he uses on an average of ten gallons a day. For those of us who live in homes or apartments with running hot and cold water our daily consumption is fifteen times

Strong dams are of major importance in any water system. They regulate rivers for flood control, navigation, and power.

that amount, or 150 gallons. We use five gallons for washing our hands and faces, for shaving and brushing our teeth. Every time we take a bath, we draw an average of twenty-five gallons Each time the toilet is flushed, another four gallons go down the drain. Then there are the modern water-gulping household appliances — air conditioners, garbage disposal units, automatic dishwashers, and home laundries.

Household use is, however, only a small fraction of our water requirement. To grow the food we need, our individual ration of irrigation water comes to almost 800 gallons a day. (Some scientists feel this is far too low a figure.) Our individual share of industry's quota is about 900 gallons. Add these up and it turns out that for each and every one of us in the United States, for each and every day, we must have available at least 1850 gallons of water. In a year, this means a total of well over half a million gallons or perhaps even more.

And it is a staggering fact that, as our individual needs keep mounting, the number of individuals keeps growing. Where are we to find enough water — enough of this primary resource for which there is not and cannot be a substitute?

The answer to this tough question depends in part on our ability to find ways of increasing the amount of usable water at our disposal. There are three general methods of bringing this about and we will need to develop all of them. The first is to use our existing sources more efficiently; the second is to find new ones; the third is to clean up our existing sources.

Stopping needless consumption of water is an immediate and a sure way of increasing water supplies. New York City alone wastes some two hundred million gallons per day because of leaks and extravagant flow.

Another possible way of increasing existing supplies is to cut down losses due to evaporation from lakes and reservoirs. One experimental method, imported from Australia, is the spreading and floating of a thin layer of acetyl alcohol on the surface of the waters. The United States Bureau of Reclamation, after extensive tests, believes that the chemical is not harmful to plant or animal life. However, the effectiveness of alcohol in cutting down on evaporation losses remains an open question.

Still another technique that is being tried in regions where water is scarce is to change the vegetative cover, using plants that have low evaporation and transpiration losses in place of those with high losses.

Then, we may stretch present supplies through increased re-use of water, particularly when it comes to industrial operations. Here is an example: It takes sixty-five thousand gallons of water to produce a single ton of steel. In the early '40's, the Sparrow's Point plant of the Bethlehem Steel Company, near Baltimore, Maryland was desperately short of the required water. The City of Baltimore had none too much water for its own growing needs, but did have one of the most efficient sewage treatment plants in the country. Presently, the steel mill's water demands were met by piping outflowing water from the city's sewage treatment plant directly to Sparrow's Point, thirteen miles away. Through this cooperation, the city and the steel plant were able to expand together without competing for the limited water supply.

In regard to the discovery and development of new sources, the most obvious way, as in California, is to channel water from where it is plentiful to where it is scarce, no matter what the obstacles or the distance or the cost.

There is a hope, too, of eventual weather modification, the coaxing of clouds to drop their burden of rain in the right quantity, at the right place, and at the right time. So far, the method is greater in hope than in fulfillment.

Most promising of all experimental methods is *desalination*, removing the salt from ocean or brackish water. From the seemingly limitless sea, we are now beginning to tap a seemingly limitless supply.

Lumbermen are not the only ones who have added to soil erosion. This badly eroded area is over-grazed range land.

At present, however, desalting is much too costly, and most arid areas too far from such water sources. Nevertheless, science may some day make obsolete the ancient mariner's tragic wail, "Water, water everywhere — nor any drop to drink."

The separation of the water from the salt is simple in principle. It can be done by distillation — evaporating the briny liquid, condensing and collecting the salt-free vapor. Or it may be done by freezing — allowing ice to form and then removing and melting the mineral-free solid. Then there are more complicated methods. One such process is called *electrodialysis*. In this method, the salt removal is accomplished by means of an electric current and plastic membranes.

In 1961, Congress authorized seventy-five million dollars to be spent over a six-year period for research and for demonstration desalination plants. Five such installations in Texas, California, North Carolina, South Dakota, and New Mexico are already in operation, each using a different method or modification. The government is finding out by actual operation how efficient the various conversion processes are. Private industry is also being encouraged to enter the field. The costs must be brought down in order to make the de-salting of water an economically feasible way of adding to our stock.

Perhaps the most important method of increasing and improving our supply of usable water is to clean up our pollution-clogged water courses. In days to come, this water will have to be used and reused again and again. The late Senator Robert S. Kerr of Oklahoma once jokingly suggested that we symbolize the clean-up task by a mermaid with a broom. It is evident that you and I and countless others in your town, and my town, and every other town will have to come to the mermaid's assistance if clean water, and enough of it, is to be ours —at the turn of a tap.

But clearing the waters is only part of our clean-up job. Quite as vital to our existence is the air that envelops us. Perhaps we had better take an upward look, for it seems that the canopy above our heads is also in need of sweeping.

5 / A Breath of Fresh Air

The day was an ordinary Tuesday morning in the fall of 1948. The place was Donora, an industrial town in Pennsylvania, a little to the south of Pittsburgh. On this day, as on most others, the harsh silhouettes of the town's wire plant and its zinc-producing plant were softened by the morning haze that hung over the countryside. There was nothing unusual or disturbing about this phenomenon, for the wind could be counted on to blow the smoke and fumes away. But this particular day — October twenty-sixth to be exact — there wasn't a breath of wind. The dead calm, added to what meteorologists call a temperature inversion, remained all that day and the next and the next as the fog piled up forming a thick, almost motionless smudge of smoke. Presently, the mills had completely vanished from view, and it was just barely possible to see the stacks. The air had a sickening reek, almost a taste, of sulfur dioxide, the throat-scratching gas given off from the zinc plant.

The town's doctors were suddenly swamped with patients, old and new. One physician described his experience in these words, "I was worried but wasn't bewildered. It was no mystery — it was obvious — all the symptoms pointed to it — that the fog and smoke were to blame. I didn't think any further than that. As a matter of fact, I didn't have time to think or wonder. I was too busy. My biggest problem was just getting around. It was about impossible to drive. I even had trouble finding the office. McKean Avenue was solid coal smoke. I could taste the soot when I got out of the car, and my chest felt tight. On the way upstairs, I started coughing and I couldn't stop. I kept coughing and choking until my stomach turned over. I just made it to the office on time. . . . After a while, I gave myself an injection of adrenalin and lay back in a chair. I began to feel better. I felt so much better I got out a cigar and lighted up. That practically finished me. I took one pull and went into another paroxysm of coughing. . . . Then I heard the phone ringing. I guess it must have been ringing off and on all day long. . . . I didn't have the strength to answer it. . . ."

The doctor's words bring to life an episode that was a disaster. Almost half of Donora's twelve thousand residents were made ill and twenty died as a result of the excessive air pollution. Eight hundred domestic animals, too, lost their lives during the three-day period.

But Donora is not unique. London has had a number of incidents in which lethal "black fogs" were held responsible for the snuffing out of lives, three hundred in the winter of 1948, four thousand in 1952, one thousand in 1956, an estimated three hundred and forty in 1962. Almost every winter has brought an added toll. Death, both in London and Donora, came mostly to people suffering from lung and heart diseases. Indeed, the veteran bronchitis patients in London clinics served almost as the miners' canaries mentioned in an earlier chapter — the patients felt discomfort hours before others noticed a smog episode was at hand.

Though sick people are the ones who suffer most during periods

In Donora, Pennsylvania, the haze and smog created by industrial pollutants caused an infamous "episode."

of severe air pollution, the evidence keeps piling up that healthy people, too, can be made miserably ill. Most striking is the case of United States servicemen stationed in Yokohama. They and their families were periodically stricken with an asthma-like illness that required medical care. It is believed by some authorities that these attacks were due to the industrial smokes that were blown over the Americans' living quarters when the wind came from a certain direction.

Smoke illness and the "choking death" (a name given to the killing disease that in 1930 claimed sixty-three lives in the Meuse Valley of Belgium) are startling examples of the danger that lurks in excessively polluted air. But what about ordinary air, the air that you and I breathe every day in our own particular town? Is our air clean enough? Is it safe enough? For today? For tomorrow?

To answer these questions, we must first of all know what pollutants we are breathing. The most obvious impurities are the visible ones — dust and smoke. Let us start with these. You might find it interesting to take a rough measure of the dustfall in your neighborhood. To do this, simply place a clean bucket, about a quarter full of water, on an unprotected elevation at least six inches above the ground. The solid particles that collect on the surface after a day's exposure will give you an idea of the dust that settles down on a very small area in the course of twenty-four hours. You might want to leave your bucket exposed and examine it again at the end of a month. In a city like New York, the monthly dustfall, mostly soot, amounts to about seventy-five tons per square mile.

Man has been sending soot into the air ever since he learned the art of firemaking. When fuels containing carbon are used — wood or coal are examples — unburned solid particles and gases escape in smoke. In the early days, when there were few colonies of men and their settlements scattered, air pollution was no problem. Smoke and soot were quickly dispersed and lost in what seemed an infinite ocean of air.

But gradually, as cities grew, the smoke refused to vanish. Edward I passed the first British smoke abatement law in 1273, but smoke continued to plague his land. This was noted over three hundred years ago by a British reporter of the day. His pamphlet, appearing in 1661, was entitled "Fumifugium: or the Inconvenience of the Aer and Smoake of London, Dissipated. Together with some Remedies humbly proposed by J. E. Esq.; To His Sacred Majestie, and to the Parliament Assembled. Published by His Majesties Command." In the article that followed this impressive title, John Evelyn described the dark haze that enveloped the city and pointed a finger at the coal that was being burned for new manufacturing processes.

In the New World, problems of smoke developed much later. The clean air of Colonial America with its small towns, vast open spaces, and lively breezes, could still be admired by travelers from the Old Country. A century after John Evelyn's time, a Britisher, the Reverend Andrew Burnaby, wrote home from New York, "It lies in a fine climate and enjoys a very wholesome air." But in 1953, a smog episode in that same New York was held responsible for the death of more than two hundred people. In December of 1962, the frightening story of New York City's air pollution problem was dramatically recounted on a television program entitled, "Take a Good Deep Breath of Filth."

As early as 1873, however, the medical correspondent of a leading American women's magazine, *Godey's,* had warned that the city people were breathing air that was thoroughly polluted with "organic dust" believed to consist of spores and disease-carrying germs. Our great-grandmothers were urged to wage unceasing battle against dust and dirt to protect the health and even the lives of their families.

At about this same time, men from both sides of the ocean — a Mr. Spence in England and the Reverend Mr. Gibsone in America — made the seemingly fantastic suggestion that smoke be discharged into sewers instead of being spewed into the atmosphere. Today, air pollution problems have become so severe in so many places around the world that an "air sewer" no longer seems a completely ridiculous or harebrained proposal. In fact, in smog-harassed Los Angeles, half-serious thought has been given to a kind of atmospheric sewer system which captures pollutants at their sources and then conducts the offenders to common points for processing.

In general, other simpler methods of air purification can still be effective, at least for the time being. These methods involve the elimination of solid particles, formed for the most part, by the incomplete burning of fuels. When people are enough concerned, they

can wage a successful battle against these solid air pollutants. The citizens of Pittsburgh and St. Louis, by restricting the use of soft coal and by substituting cleaner burning fuels, began to shake their cities free of the grey shrouds that dimmed daylight, damaged vegetation, blackened buildings, and smudged linens. The enforcement of laws requiring the installation inside industrial stacks of precipitators, devices that catch solid particles before their escape, helped to keep excessive smoke from reaching the air. What the residents of Pittsburgh and St. Louis saved in cleaning and electric light bills more than compensated for any increase in fuel outlay. And how does one measure the worth of the lifting of spirits that accompanied the lifting of the smoke?

But the struggle for clean air is not finished in either city, for like all large metropolitan areas, Pittsburgh and St. Louis still sustain undesirably high levels of air pollution. This continued fouling of the atmosphere comes from industrial processes both old and new, from increased use of motor vehicles, and from the many other sources associated with fast-growing areas.

The tale of the two cities described is undramatic compared to the story of a far western city and its attempt to clear the murky haze from its once famed skies. The Los Angeles basin on the coast of Southern California has a gentle climate but lacks good ventilation. The basin is hemmed in on three sides by mountains and on a fourth by the steady pressure of cool air from the Pacific. Hot air from the Mojave Desert flowing over the mountains overrides the cool air, forming an upside-down atmosphere called a temperature inversion. Such was the atmospheric condition of Donora on the days of its fateful "episode." The Los Angeles area suffers from temperature inversions some 260 days each year.

Steel furnaces belched unwholesome smoke into the air (above) until electric precipitators were successfully installed in the stacks (below).

Southern California has a gentle climate but very bad ventilation as seen by the smog in the famed Cajon Pass.

The Spanish explorer, Rodriguez, first noted the effects of this atmospheric quirk when he surveyed the coastline of southern California in 1542. On a bright October day, he dropped anchor in what is now called San Pedro Bay. To his surprise, he beheld mountain peaks in the distance but could not see their bases though there seemed to be no solid obstacles in the way. He noticed, too, that smoke from Indian fires started to rise perpendicularly into the calm air, and then, instead of rising further, spread out over the valley. Rodriguez was so impressed by this phenomenon that he jotted it down in his diary and named the spot "The Bay of Smokes."

The Spanish explorer had seen an example of the way in which man-made atmospheric pollution can be trapped in stagnant air. But no one paid heed to the significance of his observation. Four centuries later, residents of the ever-growing city of Los Angeles were experiencing their first daylight dim-out. The tears, coughs, and sneezes brought on by the appalling smog were followed by outraged demands to do something.

The "do something" campaign was launched in 1947 by a Los Angeles newspaper. The *Times* brought Raymond Tucker, then the leading air pollution expert in the country, to the smog-plagued city from his work in St. Louis. His survey report was the first big gun fired in a battle that is still being waged. Immediate strategy consisted of the prompt formation of the Air Pollution Control District with power to act and to act fast.

In other parts of the country, soot from the incomplete burning of coal had been the chief enemy of clean skies. Los Angeles, however, burned practically no coal. Thus, for the first time, air pollution was proved to be a problem that could not be completely equated with ordinary smoke.

The Air Pollution Control District immediately ordered industry to install filters, blowers, and scrubbers in its factories, and dust precipitators in its stacks, to eliminate all possible solid waste products before they reached the air. But the smog did not lift. Sulfur fumes from the large oil refineries were next believed to be the culprits. The petroleum companies spent six million dollars installing sulfur-recovery equipment. The smog continued to sting and smart. All forms of outdoor incineration were banned, from the demolition of auto bodies to rubbish and leaf burning. Still no relief in sight.

Finally another set of villains was discovered through the remarkable detective work of Professor A. J. Haagen-Smit of the California Institute of Technology. The Professor suspected that the ozone found in the air over Los Angeles might have some connection with smog. This ozone, a highly reactive form of oxygen, is produced by the action of California's sunlight on the ordinary oxygen of the air.

After a long series of experiments, Dr. Haagen-Smit mixed a little ozone with the waste gases of automobile exhausts. In a flash, he had reproduced in the laboratory the identical tear-provoking, throat-searing witches' brew that hovered outside his window. Ironically, what triggered the photochemical reaction that dimmed the Los Angeles sun was none other than the famous sunshine itself!

Identifying the new offenders was an important part of the battle, but no one knew how to continue the fight. Hundreds of thousands of cars flooded the streets and freeways of the area, and the number

Downtown Los Angeles has trouble with smog, but it is just part of an air pollution problem that is county wide.

kept mounting every day. How could the smog-producing exhaust gases from this growing army of cars be kept from reaching the air?

Actually only a small fraction of the exhausts emitted by automobiles from their tail pipes or vented through their crankcases are the troublemakers. The modern internal combustion engine is highly, but not one hundred percent, efficient. When a car is running, the gasoline should, theoretically, be burned to pure water and ordinary carbon dioxide, but actually, even a perfectly tuned automobile engine wastes a little fuel — about fifteen percent on the average. (Diesel and propane-gas engines for buses and trucks, as well as the still experimental gas-turbine engine are no more efficient.) In addition, cars emit much more of the highly poisonous carbon monoxide than unburned gasoline — generally four or five times as much.

Research directed at solving the auto exhaust problem was gradually undertaken by the automobile manufacturers and by others. A few promising anti-pollution devices have finally gotten beyond the experimental stage. The first general kind relies on the direct control of tail-pipe exhausts. In one type, a catalyst in the muffler causes the incompletely burned hydrocarbons and the deadly carbon monoxide in the exhaust to undergo complete burning before reaching the air. A direct flame accomplishes the same purpose in another type of tail-pipe control.

Then there is the simple and relatively inexpensive device called a *blow-by*. When an auto engine is running, small amounts of unburned hydrocarbons in the fuel leak past or blow by the pistons, enter the crankcase, and eventually escape to the air. The blow-by consists of a tube that returns these emissions from the crankcase back to the engine for burning. About thirty percent of all the harmful hydrocarbons emitted by the car may be removed in this manner.

It is an encouraging fact that, beginning in 1963, all automobile manufacturers have voluntarily furnished each new car with a blow-by. As for tailpipe devices, four have recently been tested and approved in California. It is required that, by 1966, all new cars in

This "blow-by" is typical of certain devices being used to check the harmful gases that cars release into the air.

the state be thus equipped. Old cars are given somewhat more time.

Is California doing enough? Dr. Haagen-Smit is not too optimistic. He says, "The haze is not as thick as five years ago; plant damage less, alerts not so frequent and do not last for so long a period. The measures of the Control District have held us back from disaster, even made conditions a little better — but will have to achieve a miracle if they banish smog in Los Angeles' booming future."

Meanwhile, short of a miracle, a number of more prosaic possibilities are being explored. The fuel companies are working on a gradual alteration in gasoline composition, cutting down its most active smog-making ingredients. But even a small change involves huge outlays for new oil refinery equipment.

Automobile manufacturers are studying a modification of basic engine design to eliminate the escape of hydrocarbons. One company is revamping the old-fashioned electric car used by gentlewomen of a past era. Engineers have succeeded in making a model that can reach a speed of fifty-five miles an hour and can travel eighty miles before the batteries need recharging. The perfecting of the promising new "fuel cell" may eventually provide a far more efficient battery. But even more significant may be the car powered by a gas turbine engine. Experimental models are even now being evaluated. Fortunately, the air polluting potential of this car-of-the-future seems to be relatively small.

There is also the possibility of an entirely different form of travel for the future. The monorail with its suspended track (to be described more fully in a later chapter) offers a kind of high speed mass transit that might be superimposed on southern California's landscape without wrecking its highway system. But could Californians be lured from their own steering wheels? Probably not, say the people who take polls, as long as times are good and freeways exist.

A recurring suggestion is the use of airplane seeding either to dispel the inversion hanging over the basin or to counteract the aerial garbage in it. Activated charcoal could no doubt soak up a good deal of the smog; but sprinkling charcoal is like scattering soot, and the cure might well turn out to be worse than the disease.

Two other suggestions are curtailing industry and restricting the number of people in the area. But these ideas seem quite unacceptable at present.

The miracle needed to solve Southern California's air pollution problem might possibly be performed through tighter and ever tighter controls. But are the people of the region going to be willing to accept such limitations? As of today, it seems unlikely.

Fifteen years ago, smog was a monopoly of Los Angeles. The people of San Francisco smiled and joked about it. Today, sobered by their own plight, the San Franciscans have demanded that an active air-pollution authority rule over their haze-filled skies.

Florida, the sunshine state, used to make wisecracks at the expense of its western rival. Today, Florida struggles with an air-pollution

Florida motorists are forced to turn on their headlights in broad daylight in order to pierce the shroud of smog.

problem of its own — a problem that seems certain to grow.

A news headline in the winter of 1962 reads, "Denver Squints at the Smog Problem." There is also the story of Washington, D.C., the least industrialized of our large cities, whose residents have endured several smog attacks similar to, though not as intense as, those of Los Angeles. And there are tales from Philadelphia, Boston, Detroit — one could go on citing instance after instance — for the list is a long one.

The Public Health Service estimates that approximately ninety percent of our urban population live in communities with air-pollution problems. In total, about six thousand of our cities and towns, small as well as large, are in need of action programs.

Industrialized sections of South America, Canada, Europe, and

Asia are also finding it harder and harder to clear their darkened skies. The problem of air pollution has indeed become a world-wide one.

In our own country, the fight for clean air started as a battle against an unpleasant and irritating nuisance. Dirty skies meant dirty linens, corroded metals, damaged crops, pock-marked buildings, low visibility, curtailed transportation, and decreased real estate values. What started as a nuisance was fast becoming a threat to the community's economic health. Gradually, it was realized that a far more serious danger might be at hand. It was known that the episodes of acute pollution in Donora, London, and elsewhere had been responsible for illness and even loss of life. But nothing was known about the possible effects of smaller doses day after day and year after year.

To get at the facts would require painstaking and long-term research. The passage by the Eighty-Fourth Congress of Public Law 159 in 1955 enabled the Public Health Service to initiate such research in its own facilities and in those of about fifty other institutions.

Two main courses of action have now been pursued, the one through statistical methods, the other by means of the laboratory. In an early study of the first kind, Donora was revisited to examine the aftermath of the 1948 episode. It was found that, in the age group twenty-one to fifty, there was a higher frequency of post-episode disease and death among those who were made ill during the disaster than among those who were not.

In another early study, one hundred and sixty-three typical metropolitan communities were examined for possible correlations between urban air and health. There followed intensive investigations of particular cities whose different sections had varying degrees of air pollution. All of these statistical studies, and many others, invariably show that people who live in cities, or sectors of cities with heavily polluted air, have more heart-and-lung disease and are more likely to die of it than people who live elsewhere.

Plants have been used to demonstrate effect of air pollution. Plant at left was grown in unfiltered air, right in filtered.

Let us now glance at a few of the studies that have used the laboratory approach. A number of tests have been set up to determine the biological and health effect of certain specific air pollutants, or mixtures of them. These studies are conducted mainly with test animals, a limited few with humans. Most of the experiments are still under way and the findings are therefore incomplete.

Here are a few examples of studies designed to test the effects of automobile exhausts: In Los Angeles, thousands of mice, rabbits, and guinea pigs in little open laboratories along the freeways are breathing the same air as humans. Other animals — controls — are breathing only filtered air. At Wayne University in Detroit, the test animals are divided into three groups. One set breathes the air that any office worker would inhale. Another has air piped to it from the traffic-laden freeway outside. A third group lives in a clean, filtered atmosphere. At the Public Health Service laboratories at the Taft

Sanitary Engineering Center in Cincinnati, test animals are put into compartments filled with a single set of pollutants — auto exhausts produced in the laboratory itself.

Some animals in all three cities are being sacrificed to study the immediate effects of continuous exposure. Others are allowed to live out their natural life spans so that investigations can be made of the more lasting effects of prolonged exposure.

Certain experiments have already yielded results. Animals exposed to the irritant oxides of nitrogen found in auto exhausts are more susceptible to pneumonia than unexposed animals. It has also been noted that the spontaneous activity of test animals is decreased in response to particular dosages and lengths of exposure to these gases. Though scientists are cautious about saying that human beings respond in the same manner, it seems natural to surmise that the health and well-being of humans may be involved.

Almost every possible air pollutant, or combination of them, is being studied. In addition to the gases in auto exhausts, substances like ozone, lead, fluorides, and aldehydes are under scrutiny. Name your poison; it is probably found in the air you breathe, and may well be the subject of special study. There are at present some two hundred research projects underway.

The body of conclusive evidence against air pollution grows more impressive as each new result is reported. One can't help wondering how much of this evidence must be piled up before we decide to act — or are we going to wait for further proof? A century ago, the pioneers in Public Health determined to take action on the circumstantial evidence that linked filth with communicable diseases such as typhoid. Water supplies were protected and wretched housing cleaned up in the belief that these measures would help. And they did. In the case of foul air, the evidence of its hazard to health is no longer circumstantial. On the contrary, there is already overwhelming proof.

The time for action on air pollution is most certainly *now*. To begin the job, reliable standards of air purity must first be established. To create such standards, one of the early steps is to find out how much of each kind of pollutant actually exists in a given region. For this purpose, the United States Public Health Service has set up a National Air Sampling Network. At eight Federal Monitoring Stations in selected cities across the nation, there is an automatic and continuous sampling and analysis of the atmosphere's seven most harmful gaseous pollutants. Elsewhere, at two hundred and fifty urban and rural sites, the Public Health Service continues the periodic air sampling program it started in 1955. And many other services are available — for the asking — to any community wishing to do something about air pollution. Furthermore, in accordance with the terms of a bill signed into law by President Johnson in December, 1963, a wholly new approach to federal participation was set in motion. Expanded research, training, and technical assistance programs; the awarding of funds to cities and states in developing their own air pollution control programs; powers of direct action in interstate abatement problems — these are among the measures that should give substantial help in the task of making the air we breathe more breathable.

Luckily, we already have natural assistance from the air itself. As with water, the self-cleansing properties of the atmosphere are generally good. Dust falls out, and water washes out a reasonable quantity of pollution. Winds and other air currents diffuse and dilute gaseous impurities quite efficiently. If we could suppress the most dangerous and obnoxious substances at their source, we would be well on our way to solving the air-pollution problem.

Our Town has already made progress in removing the filth from the water we drink. The reason is that we thought it important enough to be willing to foot the bill. The same applies to the air we breathe. We will restore it as a safe and what Shakespeare described as an "excellent canopy" only when we care enough to demand it, work for it, and pay for it.

We Americans are slowly, all too slowly, coming to grips with our problems of contaminated water and filthy air. But there is still a third type of pollution which we dare not forget or neglect. Let us, therefore, turn next to the question of land pollution, the despoiling of the earth itself, and the effort needed to keep at least part of it living and green.

6 / The Race for Open Space

Glance around you. Take a careful look. It may well be the last you will see of the wooded countryside that borders your town. The forest where you played Cowboys and Indians, where you found the first delicate flowers of spring, where you had a secret hiding place for reading or just plain possessing your soul — this magic forest will tomorrow cease to be.

Your family probably moved to the country to give you a chance to live in a wooded world. This exodus may even have been a second one in their flight from the city. The first uprooting and transplanting promised a land of streams and meadows, of brooks and woods, according to the "Paradise Valley" posters. But before you were comfortably settled, the streams were buried in concrete culverts, a row of stumps marked the work of the power saws, and the view from the picture window revealed nothing but row on monotonous row of identical picture windows blinking at each other. Traffic tie-ups, overcrowded schools, inadequate facilities and services, and your family was on the move again.

We Americans are consuming land for urban uses at a rate of one million acres a year. This means that if we continue gobbling up land at the present speed, nearly twelve thousand square miles, an area as large as Delaware and Maryland combined, will be removed from our land resource base in the span of only eight years.

Perhaps you have been under the impression that land in and around crowded metropolitan areas is all filled up. If you keep your eyes open as you drive through the city and its outskirts, you may be surprised to discover how much vacant space there really is. It is unattractive space to be sure — empty lots littered with refuse or automobile graveyards with their rusty, unburnable junk. If the vacant land used for these unsightly purposes were added up, it

Open space is often available in metropolitan areas in the form of unattractive vacant lots littered with refuse.

would make quite a lot of space. The trouble is that it can't be added up for it is scattered; and the fragmented parts are too small for profitable development. So the builders, who must make money to stay in business, *leapfrog* — first in small jumps and then in larger ones — to tracts where land is cheap and development easy.

Another reason for leapfrogging is the fact that the suburbs surrounding great cities are so often zoned to large residential lots. Within a fifty-mile radius of New York, two-thirds of the vacant land is reserved for half-acre lots or even larger ones. To erect apartments, or to build houses on smaller lots for the great numbers of families who seek inexpensive housing outside the core of the city, developers must skip over the zoned regions and reach farther and farther out into the open countryside. Thus, the helter-skelter pattern of "scatteration" spreads and spreads. And the landscape is chewed up as the green countryside is fed into the insatiable maws of the bulldozers.

There is now a wide strip of our northern seaboard extending from Boston to Washington, D.C., that has followed this sprawling pattern of development. This vast complex of cities, towns, and subdivisions, each running into the other, has been called *megalopolis,* a name originally used by the ancient Greeks for a town which they hoped would become the largest in Greece. There are other modern candidates for the title, one among them being the great manufacturing belt stretching from the northeastern seacoast through the Great Lakes region of the midwest; another the entire teeming state of California. A high proportion of the nation's wealth, both financial and human, is now concentrated in these and several other gigantic urban regions.

Megalopolis in the Peloponnesus remained a small town despite the dream of the ancients. Megalopolis, U.S.A. is today's colossal reality. And it is with this reality that we must come to grips. There is no use longing for the "good old days" when we lived on farms or in small rural villages, and when the wide open spaces of the West

offered adventure to the daring. Most of us, in the time to come, will be living in some urban-suburban community — if we are not there already. Megalopolis — for better or worse — is our new frontier, as tough as any that confronted and challenged our forefathers.

"Cut, burn, plant, destroy, move on." This was the slogan of our predecessors, those who peopled and developed our continent. Yet there were men from Washington and Jefferson on who saw beyond the immediate to a more distant goal. These men, conservationists in the true sense, were determined to leave a goodly heritage for those who were to follow.

An outstanding example of such foresight was the creation of New York City's Central Park. Well over a hundred years ago, William Cullen Bryant, editor of *The Evening Post,* took a walk in the countryside north of the growing city. It was wooded, hilly land, too rocky for much except grazing. Squatters' shacks were the only signs of human habitation. Bryant realized that this property would not remain undeveloped for long. The city had doubled in numbers in the last twenty years; it would most certainly continue to grow and spread. Already there was a shortage of *usable* open land close to where people lived. Cemeteries, of all inappropriate places, provided the main public recreation areas.

Bryant stopped in his ramble. An idea came to him. Why should not the city purchase the large, beautiful tract on which he walked, and set it apart for a central reservation? Bryant immediately started to agitate for his plan. "Buy the land now," he urged. "Ridiculous," declared the *Journal of Commerce,* going on to state that there was plenty of free countryside for people to visit, so why spend money

The air rights to the multiple bridge approaches to New York's George Washington Bridge are being used for apartments (above).

Open space in a large city like New York is at a premium, so "air rights" above highways are sold to contractors (below).

Central Park is an oasis of green growing things in the very middle of a complex city of cement, steel, and glass.

to buy it. But the original idea took hold, the politicians and their fellow citizens backed it, and the land was finally purchased in 1856, when the price was still reasonable.

Then, in 1857, Frederick Law Olmsted, the winner of the city's competition for the landscape design, and his colleague, Calvert Vaux, created a park that transplanted the joys of the country to the city. They made a virtue of the rocks, and turned the swamps into lakes. Today, New Yorkers are still climbing the rocks or enjoying a leisurely row on one of the lakes, thanks to the foresight of men who translated into action their concern for those who were to follow them.

The story of Central Park is not unique. Philadelphia has its extensive and beautiful Fairmount Park; Cleveland its Gordon and Edgewater Parks; San Francisco its Presidio, Lincoln, and Golden

Gate Parks. Then there is Milwaukee with its Whitnall Park and the magnificent drive along Lake Michigan's shore front. Another example is Minneapolis with its sixty-one miles of boulevards that encircle the city, connecting its many lakes and larger parks. The system, in addition, embraces a playground or neighborhood park for every square mile of residential area. The residents of Minneapolis are fortunate to find, conveniently close at hand, opportunities for golf, tennis, skating, baseball, swimming, and picnicking.

In Boston, it was landscape architect, Charles Eliot, who, in the 1890's expanded the idea of a "major site" to a *system* of parks and natural reservations for the whole of Boston's metropolitan area. The plan brought thirty-six separate towns and cities together under a single governing district. The sites chosen as reservations included woodlands, wetlands, and river banks, many of them connected by tree-lined drives. Eliot visualized these areas as fragments of the primitive New England wilderness, small links with the past, to be held for future generations who would otherwise be "more and more shut out from the beauty and healing influence of nature and scenery." By the 1960's, urban sprawl had extended around and beyond these reservations. And New Englanders of today, as aware of their responsibility to the future as were their forebears, have approved a new project, the acquisition of open spaces — belts of green — to separate metropolitan Boston from the other large urban centers of Lawrence, Lowell, Worcester, and Providence.

The acquiring of open spaces in and around a megalopolis is usually a difficult and expensive operation. Nevertheless, if we fail to act now, there simply won't be any useful space available at any price.

There are several ways in which public land may be acquired. The most obvious way is to buy it outright. This is appropriate if the land is to be developed and used for a park or a beach. If the open space is to be set aside for future use, it is possible to buy the land and then lease it. Future rights-of-way for the building of highways have been acquired in this manner by state governments.

A useful and ingenious tool for simply keeping space open is the purchase of conservation rights. When property is bought, the purchaser obtains a full bundle of rights in the land. But it is not always necessary to buy the complete bundle. The public can purchase a single right in a property. This is called an *easement*.

Here is the way one such plan works: Suppose a farmer owns a wooded hillside or a ravine with a flowing brook close to a new thoroughfare. The community does not buy this land outright but simply purchases from the owner an easement — the right to put up developments on a particular portion of the property or billboards on land close to the highway. By *not* exercising the right — and *not* building on the property — the state, county, or local government keeps the land open. This means that the farmer continues to cultivate his soil, and produce his food near the market, while the suburbanite benefits, too. He has the pleasure of looking out on the green meadows and yellow cornfields of a well-run farm in addition to the hillside or ravine set aside as a preserve.

There are other valuable and savable bits of landscape that we take quite for granted. We don't usually think of a golf course as scenery, but an easement might well prevent the links from having to become just another subdivision. Such land rescue would benefit not only golf enthusiasts but their non-golfing neighbors as well.

Some land may be acquired for the asking. There are individuals who volunteer — or may be prevailed upon — to deed their estates to the public. As far back as 1891, a group of energetic and farsighted citizens banded together to form the Massachusetts Trustees of Reservations. The group put on a vigorous campaign of persuasion. Today, in about thirty different areas, nearly five thousand acres, including some fine historic sites, have been saved from engulfment, and turned over to the public for enjoyment.

Then there are other private, non-profit groups that encourage the preservation, by gift or purchase, of as many different kinds of

natural areas as possible for purposes of teaching, learning, and research. One such organization, national in scope, is the Nature Conservancy. Among the areas that have been saved from destruction
and dedicated to study and enjoyment are woodlands of various
kinds; swamps, bogs, and ponds; prairies and meadows; limestone
caves and sandstone cliffs. Each habitat has its own special features,
its unique and often irreplaceable forms of life.

There are individual crusaders also, who have succeeded in preserving some small wedge of land that might needlessly have been
sacrificed to a builder's convenience. There is the story of Dr. Walter
P. Cottam, Professor of Botany at the University of Utah, who
cajoled the President of the University into giving him the use of a
gully that was slated for filling in when the new library building was
erected. "Never let 'em take the gulch!" became a slogan as the small
ravine was transformed with flowering trees and shrubs into a spot
of uncommon beauty and interest. Over the years the place has become known by the blunt, affectionate title of "Cottam's Gulch."

On a somewhat larger scale, groups of citizens in certain communities, have banded together to save their beautiful and well-
loved region from violation. Big Sur on the Monterey coast of
California is an excellent illustration. This wild and spectacular strip
of seaboard with its redwood-studded promontories, stark cliffs, and
sandy beaches lies almost midway between San Francisco and Los
Angeles. When the Spanish explorers first came upon this particular
part of the coast line they called it El Sur Grande — the Big South.
Since early days, the region has remained sparsely settled, for people
need to be hardy to withstand the howling winds, driving rains, and
rumbling quakes that occasionally shake the terrain.

By the early 1960's, encroachment was close at hand as builders
to the north and south started to erect motels and filling stations,
while tourists, in ever mounting numbers, jogged along the formerly
peaceful and still modest highway.

Architect Nathaniel Owings, and conservationist Nicholas Roosevelt realized what was in store, and decided to act. Under the leadership of these two men, a master plan for preserving the integrity and scenic beauty of the community, while at the same time providing for its orderly growth, was drawn up and finally adopted by the neighbors.

Whether or not Big Sur is permanently saved, the master plan for this rescue operation has features of usefulness to other areas. Instead of allowing the coastal highway to become a high speed freeway, it is to remain a simple and scenic two-lane road for leisurely travel. In addition, a novel device, that of open space "credits," encourages a landowner to leave open the part of his property lying on the coastal side of the highway — the most magnificent scenic area — in exchange for the right to build a specified number of extra houses, beyond the usual count allowed by zoning, on the upland side of his property.

This kind of land use, providing groups of houses with commonly-held tracts of open space, is called cluster planning. Let us examine this pattern more closely. Imagine yourself a developer who has purchased a two-hundred-acre farm on the edge of suburbia. The site is a pleasant one, with gently sloping ground, a stream that wanders through its center, and a fine stand of trees near one corner. The area is zoned to quarter-acre lots. If you followed conventional suburban design, you would cut down the trees, bury the stream in culverts of concrete, and cover almost a quarter of the land with black-top to provide necessary roads. These and other facilities, such as sewers and electric lines would be so costly you would have to skimp on the houses. And the very features that made the property attractive in the first place would be destroyed in the process.

There is, however, the alternative of cluster development, a plan by which you could save the stream and the woods as well as a goodly share of the land that would otherwise need to be sealed in asphalt. In other words, you could maintain the beauty of the site and, at the same time, materially cut your land improvement costs.

In addition, by grouping your houses together, you might find it possible to construct a few extra homes without exceeding the number permitted for the tract. With all the savings effected, you could well afford to contribute the rest of the land, as open space, to the entire community.

There are, however, some real headaches connected with the cluster plan. Who is going to clean up soda bottles from the community creek? Are the home owners going to be willing to assume responsibility for the maintenance of the commonly-shared greenery? Will there be sufficient buyers for this new kind of development?

"New" is perhaps not the right word to use, for the cluster planning idea is not really a new one. It was part of Ebenezer Howard's plan for England's original Garden City. The idea did not take thorough hold in America, except in isolated instances, as in Radburn, New Jersey; Baldwin Hills, California; the Greenbelt towns; and in a handful of others. Today, however, developers, planners, and community planning commissions are taking a fresh look at this pattern of development, and are beginning to experiment with cluster designs of their own. Big Sur, as we have seen, is one example. There are many others.

Five Fields in Lexington, Massachusetts, a delightful example, is an eighty-acre development that takes its name and rural character from the farmers' fields whose stone walls remain undisturbed. The partially wooded and gently rolling landscape has not been subdivided in the monotonous, conventional way. Rather, the houses have been set in the landscape with casual grace. Instead of back yards, there are open fields to be shared and enjoyed by all.

But clustering is only a small item in the planning that has to be done in regard to larger open spaces, both in and near our communities. This planning is essential if we are to meet the needs of the future — a future that keeps turning out to be closer than we think. Suppose we project ourselves into that future — the day after to-

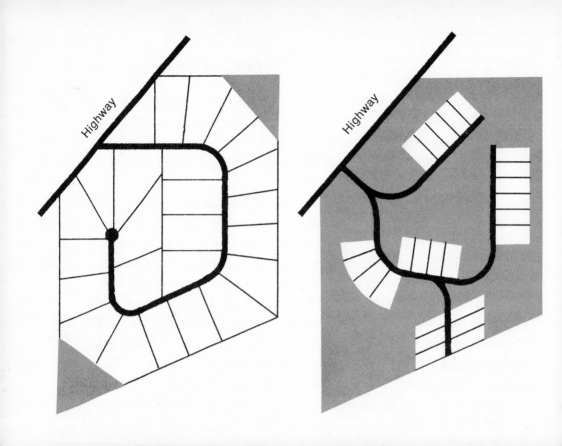

morrow and the day after that — and try to imagine what will be our needs for open space, and what kinds of open space we will need.

The United States Department of Agriculture states that though we will need fewer acres of cropland in the next decade or two (we keep growing more produce on less acreage), we will need more acres in pasture and range land for dairy goods and meat, and more acres for special uses. These uses include urban areas, recreation, roads, reservoirs, and power lines. By the year 2000, urban land needs alone are expected to double.

In 1958, Congress established the O.R.R.R.C. — Outdoor Recreation Resources Review Commission — and charged it with responsibility for determining both the outdoor recreational needs of the American people and the availability of suitable sites for today, for 1976, and for the year 2000.

The Commission estimated that by the turn of the twentieth century, while our population will have *doubled*, the demand for outdoor recreation will have *tripled*. The reasons for this intensive demand for the outdoors may be found in the fact that we keep adding to our leisure time, to our incomes, and to our facilities for getting about and going places. The Commission discovered during the course of its three-year study that the simple activities — driving and walking for pleasure, swimming and picnicking — lead the list of outdoor activities in which Americans participate. This is generally true regardless of income, education, age, or occupation.

Other findings of the Commission will not surprise you, as for example the one that outdoor opportunities are most urgently needed in and near metropolitan areas where most people are, and where most usable open spaces are not. To complicate matters, many of

Diagrams (above) illustrate use of land. On left, non-clustered houses; on right, clustering maintains beauty of site.

Five Fields, an example of cluster planning, sets the houses into the woods and fields with casual grace.

our public agencies, over the years, have been faced with a lack of funds for acquiring new areas or developing old ones.

The Commission's recommendations to meet the crisis resulted in prompt and affirmative action in Congress. In 1962, a Bureau of Outdoor Recreation, with over-all nationwide responsibility, was established under the Department of the Interior. The broad function of the new agency is to consider the needs of the American people for all phases of outdoor recreation: within cities, in rural areas, and throughout the country. To this end, the Bureau provides guidance and assistance on the Federal, State, and local levels, as well as on the private sector.

First things must come first, and it is no wonder that early efforts have been directed toward land acquisition while there is still land to be had.

In 1963, we Americans were the fortunate possessors of thirty-one National Parks, each an example of superb natural beauty. It all started ninety years earlier, in 1870, when a group of outdoorsmen met around a campfire in the Yellowstone area. They had journeyed to this wild western country to authenticate the yarns that mountain men spun about the fabulous scenery and astonishing natural wonders of the region. The tales, which they had thought to be tall, proved to be true, and the group immediately wanted to organize a private corporation to exploit the territory. One man spoke up in opposition — Cornelius Hedges, a judge from Helena, Montana. He talked quietly and movingly, declaring that such an extraordinary natural area ought not be developed as private property, but should rather be held in trust for all the people. Justice Hedges convinced

Yellowstone's Old Faithful geyser, which spouts scalding water every hour, has been a National Park attraction for many years (above).

The Oregon sand dunes — with the Pacific Ocean in the distance — are an example of a proposed National Park (below).

the others who, on their return to civilization, pressed for the idea. In 1872, Yellowstone Park was set aside as a public "pleasuring ground for the people" — our first National Park.

By 1963, thirty additional Parks as well as one hundred and seventy National Monuments and other historic sites had been established under the supervision of the National Park Service. And in 1963 there were one hundred and two million visitors to the National Parks, a gain of about thirteen percent over 1962, the preceding record year. In the face of this growing avalanche of visitors, how is the beleaguered Park Service to maintain our National Parks "in such a manner and by such means as to leave them unimpaired for the enjoyment of future generations"?

Part of the answer is to set more land aside. As of today, Congress, supported by the public, is bending its efforts to save every suitable bit of our national heritage, including our vanishing shore line. For us, and for the generations to come, there will now be adventurous new experiences on the still unspoiled "Island of Time" at Point Reyes, California; the wild reaches of the Padre Island seashore off the Texas coast; the sandy beaches and dunes along Cape Cod in Massachusetts; the white dunes and sculptured boulders of Oregon's rugged coast; the Sleeping Bear Dunes and Pictured Rocks of the Great Lakes. Your children and their children may well be journeying to Utah's colorful canyon lands, the varied wonders of the Great Basin in Nevada, the prairies of central Kansas, Missouri's unsullied Ozark River, or Cumberland Island on the Georgia coast.

In addition to the National Parks of today and tomorrow, National Forests offer vast recreational opportunities. Established by Act of Congress just before the turn of the century, our country's National Forests — one hundred and fifty-one in number — are managed on the principle of "multiple use." Recreation is an important one of

Canyon Lands National Park — with its awe-inspiring Angel Arch — is on the Colorado River. National acquisition is now under proposal.

these uses; others include timber production, water supply, grazing, and wildlife habitat. These purposes are often in conflict with each other and disputes must be reconciled in the interests of "the greatest good to the greatest number in the long run." This criterion is found in a memorandum of instruction to Gifford Pinchot, the first Chief Forester of the United States, from James Wilson, Secretary of Agriculture, in 1905.

Both our National Forests and Parks are attempting to provide appropriate and adequate facilities for visitors on selected portions of the domain. A small segment of our forest and park lands, it is hoped, will always remain untouched. Brooks Atkinson, writing in the New York *Times* on June 1, 1962, states the case for wilderness in these terms: "Wilderness areas have a grander use than the preservation of certain animals and birds. They contain the materials of knowledge. They preserve records of our past and clues to our destiny. It was from primitive areas in South America and the Galapagos Islands that Darwin discovered a fact of nature that revolutionized thinking. He could never have discovered the origin of species in a bulldozed continent covered with superhighways and split-level ranch houses. Let's hope that does not become the future of our species."

To ensure a less gloomy future for our species, to keep a vestige of wilderness and unspoiled beauty for our nation, we will have to provide hundreds of other open spaces — state, county, and local — in our public and private parks and in our public and private forests and wood lots. All possible areas will need to be whipped into service, not only to take the pressure off our National Parks and National Forests but also to provide nearby places for sports and games, for fishing and boating, for picnics and overnight camping, or for just plain sitting and enjoying the out-of-doors.

To make possible this vast variety of reserved areas for a vast variety of needs and tastes, the Federal government has made funds available to all fifty states to assist them and their municipalities in the planning and development of necessary programs, and in the acquisition of land to make these plans come to life.

Several states made an early start, even before the enactment of legislation on the Federal level. New York, for example, passed an Open Space Act in 1960, when citizens went to the polls and voted to create a state debt in the amount of seventy-five million dollars, to provide moneys for land acquisition. In less than three years, the task of acquiring all kinds of available open spaces throughout the state was substantially completed.

New Jersey followed suit in 1961 with its Green Acres Land Acquisition Act which authorized a bond sale in the sum of sixty million dollars "to acquire substantial quantities of such lands as are now available and appropriate." Other states, notably Florida, Pennsylvania, Ohio, and Wisconsin are also taking action.

The State of Massachusetts, in 1961, passed an act authorizing cities and towns to establish Conservation Commissions "to promote the development of natural resources and to appropriate money therefor." In less than three years, more than half of the three hundred and fifty-one towns of Massachusetts had taken action to create such commissions. By this means, groups of citizens are starting to inventory community resources and to seek agreement on their long-term management and development. So far, this has proved to be an imaginative and effective grass-roots approach to resource problems. Connecticut, too, is experimenting with Conservation Commissions, and has passed a multi-million dollar grant-in-aid program to stimulate local initiative. New Hampshire and Rhode Island are following close behind.

Throughout the nation, there are literally thousands of special districts designed to protect and preserve the natural environment. One outstanding example is the Forest Preserve District of Cook's County, in the neighborhood of Chicago. The Preserve is composed of beautiful wooded sanctuaries with recreational facilities on their fringes. The interiors are accessible by walking, bicycling, and horse-back riding on designated trails. Teacher training programs and outdoor laboratory experiences for young people are two of the educational services offered. The fifty-thousand acre reservation is one of the oldest special districts formed to preserve forest lands lying in the path of urban expansion.

Many states, from east to west, from north to south, are on the move and are swinging into action in a variety of ways. Is yours one of the states or one of the communities that is doing something about open space? Is yours a state or community in which young people have a share in the doing?

Idaho is such a state. Every summer, one high school boy from each of Idaho's forty-four counties is selected by lot from among potential candidates to attend a work camp at the Priest Lake State Forest. The boys clear trails, plant trees, get rid of brush and debris, improve camp and picnic areas. Apparently the teenage workers have such a satisfying, as well as useful, experience that there are five times as many applicants as places. A by-product for the boys is the glimpsing of career possibilities in the field of forest service.

Newton, Massachusetts, is a community in which young people have played an active part in recreating useful open space in the heart of their congested suburban city. The space was a run-down thirty-three acre park disfigured with litter and rubbish, haunted with legends of terror. But Edmands Park, with its flowering ravines and tree-clad slopes, was a priceless potential for Newton's citizens, old as well as young.

Under the sponsorship of the Lincoln Filene Center for Citizen-ship and Public Affairs of Tufts University, a pilot program was set up in cooperation with the Newton schools. During the course of the summer seminar, whose subject was "The Dilemmas and Prospects of Urban Civilization," twenty-three high school seniors — girls as well as boys — spent part of each study and work day in Edmands Park, cleaning up the trash, rehabilitating trails, and re-creating a

To salvage this burned-out California woodland, trees will be replanted at the rate of about 700 acres a year.

shallow pond for winter skating. In addition, the students examined alternative policies and plans for the park, made recommendations to the city government for the care of the land, and alerted the whole community to the task that still lay ahead.

Hundreds of other young people, if given the opportunity, could and would help in the tremendous effort to save the open land we already possess. A Youth Conservation Corps opens exciting possibilities for a nationwide effort toward this end.

Reserving and restoring open space is indeed one of our top priorities, requiring assistance from us all. But even the most attractive open space is of small use unless it is accessible. This brings us face to face with the problem of how to unravel the presently tangled web of travel and transportation. Therefore, let us turn to the question of how, in the years to come, we may get from urban space to open space and back again with some measure of speed and comfort, without completely ruining the open space at the same time.

7 / To and Fro

Our Town and its neighbor have an important decision to make. The Village Board members, aware that traffic has become unmanageable, have agreed that a modern highway is needed as a new link between the towns. There are two alternative plans: Route A is the most direct, but will require the drainage of a coastal marsh used by waterfowl for breeding and migration; the less direct Route B runs through farm land, and will necessitate the purchase of several portions of private farms. Estimates indicate that the farm route will be somewhat more expensive than the other.

The Land Selection Committee's experts — a highway engineer, a city planner, a wildlife specialist — will need to weigh the pros and cons with care before giving their advice. Which is more valuable, they must decide, the preservation of the wetlands, of which so few are left, or the saving of the strip of farm land? How much should the dollar sign affect the choice?

Decisions regarding the location of roads, highways, or freeways are often difficult and sometimes heartbreaking. People become deeply attached to their particular bit of earth, and feel uprooted when their land, and perhaps their home itself, must be sacrificed to "the greater good." Unfortunately, there is always some property, either public or private, that must be destroyed if new roads are to be built. Furthermore, there is less and less vacant space in and around megalopolis from which to choose, and the choices become harder and harder to make.

There are some highway and expressway decisions which, if executed, would completely ruin or destroy unique natural beauties. In a number of cases, private indignation is finally channeled into organized protest. Two examples are the action groups formed to save the priceless Redwoods of Northern California and the beautiful sand dunes of Fire Island off the Atlantic shore of Long Island.

The motor age is, of course, responsible for our vastly expanded need for new roads and highways. Before the advent of the automobile, people lived close to their work, their schools, their churches, and their town halls. In general, these communal centers were within walking distance. More extensive travel was mainly by carriage, trolley, and train. As for food and other goods, these necessities and luxuries reached centers of distribution by ship and barge, by railway freight and express. Horse-drawn vehicles did the local hauling through cobblestoned streets.

With the building of a practicable internal combustion engine in the late 1800's, and the subsequent invention of the automobile — a happening that may well be within the memory of your grandparents — we suddenly found ourselves a nation on wheels. Today, private cars transport us on our myriad errands: to work, to play, to

America is a "nation on wheels," with two motor vehicles for every five persons. The crowded highways reflect this fact.

shopping center, or else on visits to friends, to the beach, to the mountains, to anywhere and everywhere.

Then there are the buses: to take students to school, to take adults to and from their work, to take travelers from city to city, from east to west, from north to south. Vast fleets of taxis take care of short local trips in town and city.

As for the flow of goods — while rail and water are usually best for handling heavy, bulky shipments going long distances, and while air freight supplies the quickest service, trucks and trailers now carry the largest share of our merchandise.

Fifty thousand companies own fleets of ten trucks or more. Service industries, in particular, depend heavily on the automobile. A single company like Bell Telephone uses some seventy thousand trucks to keep our phones in order. It is estimated that one out of every six cars on the road is a truck.

When we consider that there are approximately two motor vehicles for every five persons in the United States, the phrase "a nation on wheels" is hardly an exaggeration. Hundreds of interrelated problems need to be solved in the effort to get us, our food, and supplies to and fro, from town to town, from town to open country, from suburb to city, and, most particularly, from street to street within the city itself.

It may be helpful to compare traffic flow with the flow of water found in nature. Water, originating in countless springs, pours through brooks and rivulets into rivers which unite into mighty streams that eventually empty into the ocean. Outlying areas are the springs, roads and highways the brooks and rivers which merge into the larger freeway to converge finally on the city center. But the poor old city center is no ocean. And so, the swollen river of traffic is forced to trickle as best it can through the narrow canyons of the downtown streets. Naturally, the traffic backs up.

It was Benton MacKaye, forester and father of the Appalachian

Trail, who first made this analogy back in the 1920's, as he looked down from the top of the Times Building in New York's famous Times Square. Years later, architect-planner, Victor Gruen, using the same analogy, evolved what he called the basin theory. He suggested that we create retention basins where traffic streams merge just as we create flood control reservoirs to take care of excess water.

Victor Gruen's Fort Worth plan, in which he developed this idea, was the first attempt to revitalize the core of an important American city, essentially through solution of its traffic problem. Though the plan has not yet been carried out in the Texas city, its bold concept has helped to spark similar, though smaller, projects in other places. You will recall, for example, the new city center in the heart of Rochester, New York, described in an earlier chapter.

Gruen believes that, in order to build a retension basin for traffic, it is necessary to have a ring road with provision for parking on its periphery. His Fort Worth plan calls for such a road with six multi-

The Fort Worth Plan solves the midtown traffic problem by circling a proposed carless center with a fast roadway.

deck parking garages penetrating into the center like fingers. The greatest distance between any building and the nearest parking penetration is about six hundred feet — a two-minute walk. The inside of the ring is a protected pedestrian island from which the auto is completely banned. Thus the girdling of the center of the city by a belt highway outlines and protects the core, and provides circulation around rather than through it. Gruen explains, "The belt must be tight if downtown is not to lose its pants."

Various cities have adopted and modified the ring road area. Kansas City is one such metropolis. Its freeway loop — to be completed in 1972 — will encircle the Central Business District. The peripheral parking on one side of the city's center will bring downtown within easy walking distance of shoppers. The belt, however, has not been drawn tightly, and much automobile traffic will continue to crisscross through downtown streets.

The city of Boston is well on the way to completing its central loop which tunnels under the downtown core. In addition, Boston is now surrounded with a second and outer belt. Route 128, a modern, four-lane divided highway, replaces the heavily traveled two-lane roads of obsolete design that meandered from the city right through the business centers of its neighbors. In the days before there was rapid transportation, villages and towns were necessary stopping-off places. The traveler needed a pause to refresh himself and his horses. The automobile eliminated this necessity and put the accent on speed.

Boston's new circumferential highway, located about ten miles from the city's central business district, was the first effective high-speed route to encircle a congested metropolitan area. By its location on vacant land just outside the highly-developed areas, Route 128 bypasses the centers of neighboring towns and cities, yet is accessible to all of them.

After the Second World War, there was a great surge of interest in moving away from decay and congestion into the open countryside, but not too far away from the city. The time was ripe, and the location of Route 128 was ideal. It opened up inexpensive land near where people wanted to live and work. Attractive industrial parks, research laboratories, a university campus, and pleasant suburbs now border the landscaped highway, each point of which is only a few miles from the center of the great metropolis.

Other states, and their counties, cities, and towns are swinging into action, too. Comprehensive planning has been enormously stimulated since the passage, in 1956, of the Federal Aid Highway Act, legislation that will leave its impress on every nook and cranny of our country. The year 1972 should see the completion of a forty-one-

Modern freeways and turnpikes are intricate arrangments of under- and over-passes designed for speed and ease.

thousand-mile superhighway network, known officially as the National System of Interstate and Defense Highways. The Federal government will foot ninety percent of the bill for this multi-billion-dollar program, the biggest public works enterprise in our nation's history.

What a long road we and our cars have traveled in the last half century! In 1912, a bill to finance a system of national roads was attacked as a frivolous expenditure "for the benefit of a few wealthy pleasure seekers." Today, we are completely car-oriented, cherishing the freedom of movement that only individual transportation can give. Furthermore, we've decided to build ourselves a highway system that will keep us rolling.

The roads of tomorrow may even do the rolling for us, as we take our hands from the wheel, and allow an electronic analog computer to "command" the power steering systems of our cars. Already there is a half-mile loop of experimental highway at RCA's Research Center in Princeton, New Jersey. But whether we steer ourselves or are steered by electronics, our ever-growing numbers of motor vehicles call for vast new systems of roads and highways.

It seems that in the past we've cared more about going places than about the beauty of the roads that took us there. We've often allowed ugly billboards and garish honky-tonks to mar the splendor of the landscape. A few truckloads of trees and shrubs have not created the scenic highways we might have built had we given aesthetic considerations their due. Many of us spend a considerable portion of our time traveling on highways and freeways. Does this scenery have to be dull, mediocre, or downright ugly? Perhaps in places close to large industrial centers no alternative is left. But where the opportunity still exists, as it does in the open countryside, let us hope we have the good sense to design our new ribbons of hardtop with an eye to natural scenic beauty as well as to utility, safety, and speed.

So far, though we may have succeeded to some extent with these last three objectives, our best laid plans have proved inadequate.

Boston's Route 128, for example, has already required costly reconstruction, with added lanes and widened overpasses.

Once we leave the highways to enter the heart of almost any city, we encounter the problem of what to do with our cars. If streets and parking space were provided for all the people who own autos, there would be no room left for the city itself! John Crosby, writing in his column in the New York *Herald Tribune* has put it another way. Addressing the automobile manufacturers he quips, "If you'll take my advice, Detroit, (and you haven't about anything so far), you'll design your fall line so that the cars fold up and slip into your pocket, because that's the only space left anywhere in the world."

Even if all our automobiles were pocket size, as indeed they are not, the problem of getting into and out of our large city centers would remain unsolved. For safe travel, the relatively large spaces required between individual cars is more significant than car size. While auto design is a crucial factor in parking, it is not the answer to congested highway travel. One partial solution lies in offering and encouraging the use of a good alternative to the private car.

First among the possibilities are the railroads. Unfortunately, almost all of their antiquated and dilapidated commuter lines are in financial difficulty. Yet many suburbanites depend on this form of transportation to get to their work in the city. Others might gladly give up the frustration of traffic and non-existent parking facilities if only the commuter services were more efficient, more attractive, and less costly. Might there be some way of revitalizing these services?

Boston, among several other cities, said yes, and set to work on a demonstration project. In 1963, the state government, with the aid of Federal financing, made it possible, during a trial year, for the local railroads (and bus companies) to increase schedules and decrease fares. The results are yet unclear, but they do indicate some increase in the use of mass transportation, particularly in the less crowded hours of midday.

Other experiments, too, have met with some success. The city of Philadelphia subsidizes commuter railways, which, in consequence, now offer lower fares and better service. In addition, the city is spending more than a million and a quarter dollars over a period of six years to add new parking facilities at forty commuter railroad stations within the city limits. Most of the parking lots are free, and many a suburbanite, instead of struggling with traffic, is finding it pleasanter and cheaper to use the train.

The city of Cleveland, Ohio, has built itself remarkable new commuter facilities within the limits of the city. Rapid Transit officials describe their thirty-million-dollar transportation system as a "necklace" of high-speed welded rail, studded with fourteen beautiful stations. Green, yellow, and red semaphore lights of a two-million-dollar signal-control system sparkle between stations, while sixty-eight silver-and-blue cars flash across the length of the tracks. The trains, operating on their special rights-of-way, pass through the most congested areas of the city without touching a street, roadway, or bridge occupied by other traffic. "Feeder" buses, attractive and smokeless, transport riders directly to the Rapid Transit stations, some of which have ample parking spaces for private cars. Clevelanders are pleased with their fast, comfortable urban transit system.

As new commuter lines are built to service our large metropolitan areas, engineers and planners are increasingly confronted with the dilemma of space for the railroad tracks. Chicago has found an ingenious way of solving the problem. The modern freeway running from the center of downtown provides high-speed electric service on a right-of-way in the middle of the area between the in- and outbound auto lanes.

In addition, the chairman of the Chicago and Northwest Railroad devised a way to speed commuters on the last lap of their train journey to town. He explained, "We discovered one completely unused expressway right in the heart of the city. It is wider than most Loop streets; it is the one remaining traffic artery in downtown Chicago that is completely free of people, vehicles, stop lights, and 'No Left Turn' signs. The new expressway is none other than the Chicago River which passes within half a block of the railroad terminal. Two sightseeing cruisers now offer diesel-powered gondola service that takes the commuter downtown or back to the railroad terminal in seven minutes, at a cost of about a third of the taxi fare."

Several cities are now toying with the idea of constructing moving underground sidewalks — conveyor belts that could take people directly downtown from fringe area parking lots.

Then there are buses, with their flexibility of routing and scheduling and the possibility of increasing their speed by providing separate right-of-way bus lanes on the newer expressways. Some cities, Washington and Los Angeles for example, are at present completely dependent on this form of mass transportation for local and suburban travel.

There is another mode of rapid transit that has one great advantage over buses, taxis, and other motor vehicles. Subway or underground systems are unhampered by street traffic, and have long been a quick way of traveling through and across a large city and its outskirts. If one wants to get around New York City, for instance, the subway is by far the speediest means, though the sardine in its tin can has roomy quarters in comparison to the humans at rush hours.

Canada's first subway system rolled into operation in the spring of 1954. "Subway Day" marked the birth of a new era for the city of Toronto — the culmination of ten years of planning and four years of construction. Toronto wished to convert some of its auto drivers to transit riders. Traffic experts agreed that a highway twenty lanes wide would be required to carry, in private cars, the number of passengers transported by their new subway. Toronto delights in its swift, safe, comfortable, economical new transit system, which has not only helped to relieve traffic congestion, but has stimulated better living conditions and improved business all along the route.

In November, 1962, residents around California's San Francisco

Bay area voted to pay more taxes so that in a few years they might catch a subway under Market Street, cross the bay by tunnel, and arrive within minutes at the neighboring downtowns of Oakland or Berkeley. It is planned that trains will travel above and on the ground as well as under it. Though the system is not expected to solve all transit problems, it should loosen traffic jams, and reduce the need for more freeways and bridges. Now that the Federal government is taking up the mass transit cause with the offer of Federal aid, San Francisco officials estimate that completion of their sorely-needed rapid transit system can be speeded by three and one-half years. The target date for the opening of the seventy-five-mile system is 1971.

Among the most interesting features of the San Francisco plan are some technical innovations. Fare collection, for example. The subway rider will insert his card into an electronic machine at the turnstile, much as he uses a clock for punching time. The machine will then bill the passenger at the end of the month. Other turnstiles will collect cash fares, and there will be automatic change-making machines at suitable spots.

Subways provide one type of rapid transit, elevated systems another. But the "El" has added to the noise, dirt, and confusion of already overcrowded streets. It has darkened the homes and created slum areas for the people forced to live in its shadow. New York City has finally ripped the elevated lines out of the streets of its central section.

The 1962 World's Fair at Seattle introduced to America another kind of "El" — the Monorail. Its supporting structure is slender, and offers little obstruction to light or to traffic. The service is clean and speedy.

Actually, monorails are not new. The first was constructed more than sixty years ago in the heart of Germany's industrial Ruhr. The unique, suspended monorail, that from a distance looks like a giant centipede, has been the backbone of the region's passenger trans-

The old Third Avenue El — now torn down — added to the noise, dirt, and confusion of crowded New York streets.

portation since 1901. Traffic difficulties even then were so severe that the idea was proposed to connect the independent towns of the area by a fast railway system. The Wupper River, a small stream in a narrow valley, hemmed in by mountains, occupied the only free space available, and the only way to use that space was to erect some kind of elevated structure. Just before the turn of the century, Eugene Langen came before the public with his sensational invention — a suspended monorail. His idea was quickly accepted.

Wuppertalers are proud of their *schwebebahn* which has been serving them well for all these years. The cars are suspended below the trolley assembly which in turn is supported by sloping latticed girders that straddle the river. Some of today's monorail cars in other localities travel on top of the rails.

Los Angeles is at present building itself a monorail to whisk passengers from airport to town. The seventeen mile trip will take a brief twelve minutes. Other cities will perhaps follow suit. But monorails are not the only novel kind of transport being worked on by engineers all over the world. Some systems have two rails; some no rails at all.

One design of the future is the "Westinghouse Transit Express-

To the Germans of the Wupper Valley, the monorail is a familiar sight, though Americans saw their first in 1962.

way" using two troughs on an aerial roadway. The cars are to be light aluminum air-conditioned buckets carrying twenty passengers each. Riding silently on rubber tires, the trains will be electrically powered and completely automatic. About the only humans to be seen aboard will be the passengers.

Still another transit model of tomorrow is a wheelless, electrically-powered train invented by Christopher Cockerell of Great Britain, which will travel on a half-inch cushion of compressed air generated within the train. This *Hovertrain*, which is to move at speeds of up to three hundred miles an hour, will travel on a cement trough track to keep the cars from slipping sideways. The trough will contain part of the equipment for generating the needed electricity, the rest of the apparatus being attached to the underside of the train.

Somewhat similar to the Hovertrain is our own Ford Motor Company's *Levatrain*. It too, is supported by an air film — but this one only an eighth of an inch in thickness. The Levatrain is to run on smooth metal rails, and move forward by means of a gas turbine propeller.

Ground Effect Machines (or GEMS) obtain their lift by a cushion of air which is maintained at a pressure slightly higher than the surrounding atmosphere. This is accomplished by means of large horizontal fans. To retain the air cushion, a "curtain" is produced along the edge of the vehicle, usually by a jet of high velocity downward-directed air. This curtain may also be a sheet of water, or may actually be, at least in part, a flexible or a rigid material.

Transportation experts believe that underdeveloped nations may be the first to use ground-effect or air-cushion machines in numbers. Without man-made roads, these countries could employ the natural, already smooth highways of rivers, deserts, and marshes to fly their hovercraft. To create other relatively flat surfaces, it has been suggested that wide paths be bulldozed through the jungle, and covered with an airtight petroleum compound to kill vegetation.

By 1961, there were already in existence air-cushion vehicles of thirty-eight different designs and models. In 1962, a British vehicle weighing twelve-and-a-half tons became the first to go into active service on a nineteen-mile ferry run. Powered by four gas turbines, the vessel attained a speed of sixty knots.

Enthusiastic developers of ground effect machines even visualize their use for rapid ocean crossings. It is estimated that an atomic-powered vessel of this type might shoot across the Atlantic in half a day.

Another type of "flying" vessel is the *hydrofoil*. Its foils or struts, affixed to bow and stern, keep the hull well out of the waves, thus avoiding the pitch and roll of a conventional ship.

What makes a hydrofoil "fly"? The principle is the same as that which causes an airplane to soar. The term "foil" means a surface

Hydrofoils — super-fast boats that ride above the surface of the water on two or three wings — are among the newest vehicles.

shaped so that when it moves through air or water it develops a "lift" — a force at right angles to the direction of movement. The wing of a plane is an *air*foil; it raises a plane. In the same manner, a *hydro*foil raises a boat. As the speed is increased, the lift increases until the hull of the vessel clears the water completely.

Hydrofoils have rather an old history. More than sixty years ago, the Italian Forlanini first applied the basic hydrofoil principle to boats. Americans and Germans continued the development of these vessels. In 1956, a small fleet of hydrofoil ferries started operation between Sicily and Italy. In July, 1963, the American Hydrofoil Lines launched five twenty-four-passenger boats to come to the aid of a handful of harried New York commuters.

The first hydrofoil craft in the world designed specifically to plow

Similar to the hovertrain is the Hydroskimmer SKMR-1, which rides a foot above the ocean on a cushion of air.

the ocean was the H.S. (Hydrofoil Ship) *Denison* which made its maiden "flight" in 1962. The *Denison* is mainly a research ship whose mission it is to investigate and evaluate the operation of other large hydrofoils on the open sea.

For speed of transportation, the airplane is still the supreme conqueror of space, over land and over sea. Each year, modern aircraft beats its own speed record by performing a new miracle with time. But too often the magic-carpet flight by jet is counterbalanced by the snail-paced journey between airport and city. This is the bottleneck that must somehow be broken. Helicopters, as well as monorails, operating between airports and city centers may be part of the answer. Some cities already offer the helicopter service.

Even more promising are the new Vertical Take Off and Landing vessels, the VTOLs. These flying devices, holding about fifty passengers, are lifted straight up into the air and then go charging off horizontally at some five hundred miles-per-hour. No airports are needed; a big city can be dotted with small landing pads instead. At present, VTOLs are being constructed for military trials only, but we know that the military plane of yesterday is the passenger carrier of today.

In a future not too distant, there may be still another revolution in transportation history. The idea is one that has intrigued inventors from the time that cars and airplanes came into use. Prototypes have already been built of an autoplane, a combination land-air vehicle which is described as "safe to use in congested areas and taking little more skill to operate than that now possessed by the average driver." It is hard for us to visualize the impact of such a revolution on our cities, our suburbs, our countryside, our highways and airways, and our design for living.

Whatever the future holds by way of invention and innovation, all we can hope to do is to plan sensibly for today and for what we believe will be the needs of tomorrow. In the area of transportation, this means primarily that we must design integrated systems, using all the available modes of travel — over, under, and on the land; over, under, and on the sea; and through the air.

In order to use these varied methods of transportation in a synchronized, complementary, and harmonious way, we will need the thinking not only of engineers and planners, but of landscape architects, graphic artists, sociologists, and economists. We will need to listen, also, to the voices of ecologists, the scientists who can tell us what we are doing to our environment — our habitat — as we blithely, and often thoughtlessly, go about the business of changing the face of the earth.

One other caution: We can no longer think of Our Town in isolation, for all towns and all the spaces between and beyond them are linked in a web of relationships. Transportation is but one of the strands. To trace a few of the others will be the theme of the next chapter.

8 / Beyond Our Town

The peculiar mark — there it was again. The scientist noticed it with surprise and ran the infrared test once more to be sure he hadn't been mistaken. Yes, there it was — the identical wiggle on the spectrograph — unmistakably clear.

The test was a routine one; the scientist had performed it with dozens of samples of water sent for analysis to the Robert A. Taft Sanitary Engineering Center in Cincinnati, Ohio. Just a week before, the unusual wiggle had shown up in a sample from St. Louis, and here it was again, in the water of New Orleans.

"Detectives" from the United States Public Health Service finally succeeded in solving the mystery of the marks. The culprit was discovered to be a single chemical from a St. Louis factory. Some of the waste substance, used exclusively in this one factory, had traveled hundreds of miles down the Mississippi River without undergoing any change. Although the chemical — called *o*-nitrochlorobenzene —

had been diluted by the billions of gallons of water pouring daily past the city of New Orleans, there was enough of the substance in a sample quart to be clearly identified. The chemical was one of an increasing number — running into the hundreds — "whose toxic nature indicated that it should not be present in any concentration," said the U.S. Public Health Service. The plant voluntarily stopped discharging it.

This true story demonstrates dramatically that St. Louis is not, in the words of John Donne "an Iland intire of it selfe" but "part of the maine" just as every city, village, and hamlet is linked to others through its water, its air, its land, and its living things. We of today are slow in reaching this understanding, for we like to think we are sufficient unto ourselves.

In November, 1963, more than five million fish were found dead with peculiar symptoms, in the Mississippi River basin. Chemists traced the cause to endrin and dieldrin, found in the fish. These pesticides, used for spraying crops of sugar cane, cotton, and corn, had evidently drained into the rivers from the farmlands of Missouri, Arkansas, Tennessee, Mississippi, and Louisiana. Inadequate waste-disposal practices of the pesticide industry may well have been an additional cause of the lethal pollution of the waters.

Let us borrow another example from the Mississippi River. For many decades, people at its mouth built dikes or levees to protect themselves against ever-recurring floods. When the river persisted in overflowing its embankments, the dikes were built higher. Finally, thoughtful people began to realize that if they went upstream and prevented the waters from rushing down, the river would not rise so high when it approached its destination. What had to be done was to "store" the water upstream by proper soil and water management. The planting of trees and the plugging of gullies were two

Large-scale regional planning turned this gullied land (above) into a productive forest area (below) in less than twenty years.

ways of holding the water in the soil, thereby staying the deluge before it started. Only by a combination of upstream water storage and downstream damming could the waters of the great river be brought under control.

Every river is part of a still larger whole — a watershed. What exactly does the word watershed mean? When you were a small child you probably had a favorite mud puddle in which you liked to play. The part of the yard or street from which the water flowed to form the puddle was its watershed. Or take the example of the small stream on which you floated your toy boats. Water from a few acres running downhill drained into that creek. This and others like it ran into a still larger stream. These little watercourses and the land they drained constituted the watershed of the larger river into which they flowed. Small and medium-sized watersheds make up the larger ones. The Mississippi River, for example, drains a watershed of about one and a quarter million square miles.

Over the years, people have begun to see the wisdom of thinking and planning in terms of a whole watershed rather than attempting to deal with isolated segments. By the early 1930's, a number of states and the Federal government itself were committed to vast experiments in the field of regional planning. This kind of planning includes not only the management of the waters of a region but of the many interrelated factors of the total environment. Regional plans center around people, the people who live in the region.

Before taking a closer look at any of these major enterprises, let us stop to examine an early concept of the process itself. Here is a definition written some years ago for the Encyclopedia Britannica: Regional planning is "the term used to describe a comprehensive ordering of the natural resources of a community, its material equipment, and its population for the purpose of laying a sound physical basis for the good life."

The Encyclopedia goes on to illustrate the method of regional planning by taking a single aspect of regional life, the management of a forest for lumber. The area selected in this illustrative plan lies between the Cascade Range and Puget Sound in the state of Washington. The given segment— about the size of Rhode Island — is one vast forest except for the mountain barriers and the narrow strips of agriculture along the river.

If this area were exploited by all too common methods, the forest would be cut over in one operation, the workers would have only temporary employment, and there would be no provision for natural reforestation. In other words, the forest would be "mined," and the resulting devastation would make the area unfit for further activity.

Under a plan for the region, a forest-working plan in this instance, the entire area is divided into six "cutting blocks," each block to be lumbered within a ten-year period, and the logs hauled to a central saw mill. By the time the last block has been cut over — a process taking sixty years — the first is ready to be lumbered again, for the forest is continually helped toward self-renewal by making natural reforestation possible. The central mill and the housing provided for foresters and lumbermen are permanent installations rather than temporary and make-shift ones.

This simple forest plan is a prototype of planning. It will help us to distinguish important features of a sound regional plan for any given geographic area. First, there is the discovering and inventorying of the region's natural resources, then the development of a sound economic life based on the wise management of those resources. Finally, there is provision for relatively permanent homes, not to mention the social facilities and amenities that go to the creation of a good life for the people of the region.

Now let us turn again to a large watershed, and to an experiment that has become a great world laboratory as well as a great regional planning and development project.

If you had been a young person living in the Tennessee Valley

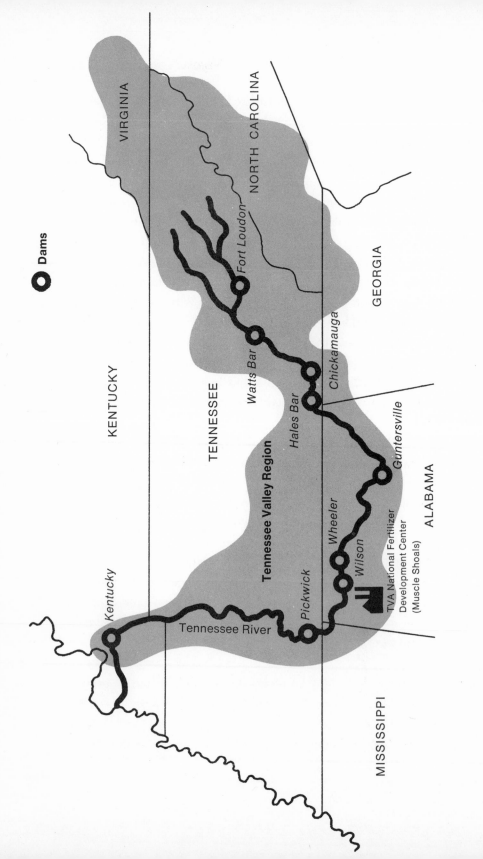

● Dams

VIRGINIA

NORTH CAROLINA

GEORGIA

KENTUCKY

TENNESSEE

ALABAMA

MISSISSIPPI

Kentucky

Tennessee River

Pickwick

Wilson

Wheeler

TVA National Fertilizer
Development Center
(Muscle Shoals)

Guntersville

Hales Bar

Chickamauga

Watts Bar

Fort Loudon

Tennessee Valley Region

Map of the Tennessee River — which winds in and out of seven states — indicating the dams in the TVA system.

during the depression of the early thirties, the income of your family might have been little more than one hundred dollars a year. As with so many others, your folks may well have crept back to the valley after their brief fling in the north, a migration caused by the lure of job opportunities in the days of industrial boom.

But the boom was over and hard times had set in, with the usual accompaniment of joblessness, hunger, and want. And yet, the Tennessee Valley was one of the nation's richest in fertility and economic possibilities. Besides enormous hydroelectric potentialities, there were metals, coal and petroleum, ceramic materials, lumber, and ingredients for fertilizers, in addition to essentially rich farmland. With its wealth of undeveloped resources, the Tennessee Valley was in the paradoxical position of being a deficiency area in the midst of potential abundance.

When the depression hit, there followed years that seemed without hope. But the idea of regional planning was in the air, and at long last, on May 18, 1933, Congress passed, with Franklin D. Roosevelt's approval, the organization of the Tennessee Valley Authority.

In proposing the TVA to Congress, President Roosevelt stated that the new Federal authority should be charged with the broadest duty of planning for the proper use, conservation, and development of the natural resources of the Tennessee River drainage basin and its adjoining territory for the general social and economic welfare of the people of the valley and of the nation as a whole.

What happened next must have seemed a miracle to the two million people directly affected and to the additional millions on adjacent land. Had you been there, you would have witnessed earthshaking changes — the building of giant dams; the flooding of land for reservoirs; the curbing, harnessing, and cleaning of the great muddy river for cheap electrical power, for water supply, for navigation, and for the pleasures of boating, swimming, and fishing. If your home had been in the path of these activities, TVA would have helped you to resettle on another and better farm, or perhaps in the

burgeoning, newly-planned town of Norris, Tennessee.

A bright day had indeed dawned in the Valley. Persuaded and encouraged by TVA, the people of the region gradually found themselves able to plan their own future with the technical assistance of experts. And that future included the elimination of diseases such as malaria and hookworm. That future also meant prosperous farming, flourishing new industry, a thriving recreational trade, better schools, better communities, *and* better lives. In addition, that future represented continuing research to develop to the full every possible resource for the well-being of the people and of those who were to come after them.

And what of the present — the glowing future of all those yesterdays? An item appearing in a New York newspaper in May, 1963, tells a small part of the story. Within the TVA region lies the National Fertilizer Development Center at Muscle Shoals, Alabama. While producing a liquid fertilizer designed to speed plant growth, scientists at the Center discovered that the substance was also an excellent fire-fighter. Today, liquid ammoniated phosphate snuffs out dozens of blazes in the Great Smokies, the Blue Ridge mountains, and the Alleghenies to the north. As a bonus, the fire extinguisher-fertilizer stimulates the recovery of charred areas by speeding the re-growth of vegetation. This small news item gives emphasis to the continuing research, discovery, and application that have always marked the progress of TVA.

The Tennessee Valley project was, and indeed still is, an experiment of the first magnitude. Engineers and dignitaries from almost every nation in the world have come to observe, to enjoy, and to learn, and have gone home eager to introduce modified TVA's into their own regions. Having found at first hand that it could be done, people from even the most deprived areas have been fired with the

Badly eroded land in the Tennessee Valley 27 years ago (above) has been improved by TVA experiments in regional planning (below).

TVA's experimental fertilizer plant at Muscle Shoals where scientists accidentally discovered an excellent fire-fighter.

hope that they could do it, too.

Thirty years after the birth of TVA, David E. Lilienthal, its former chairman, said that he believes TVA's most significant accomplishment is not its production of cheap electric power, but its demonstration to the world that regional development can best be achieved by involvement of the people of the region themselves. "After thirty years," Mr. Lilienthal said, "the people of seven states — a generation of them — feel that TVA is something that *they* have built, as indeed it is."

Though we Americans have never duplicated the organizational set-up of TVA, we have tried a number of variations on the theme. In the case of the Tennessee River Valley project, a Federal corporation, the Tennessee Valley Authority, had the final responsibility.

Another form of watershed authority is represented by the Delaware River Basin Compact. This agreement, signed into law by President Kennedy on September 27, 1961, is a compact between the states of Delaware, New Jersey, New York, the Commonwealth of Pennsylvania, and the United States of America "for the planning, conservation, utilization, development, management, and control of the water and related natural resources of the Delaware River Basin, for the improvement of navigation, reduction of flood damage, regulation of water quality, control of pollution, development of water supply, hydroelectric energy, fish and wildlife habitat, and public recreational facilities."

This comprehensive, multiple purpose plan, serving a vast region — including the giant cities of New York and Philadelphia — represents years of study, research, and consultation by federal and state agencies and by groups of citizens. The Maxwell Graduate School of Syracuse University was entrusted with the task of recommending the organizational structure best fitted to accomplish the physical plan drawn up by the U.S. Corps of Engineers. The first phase of the vast program, planned to serve an eventual forty-two million people, is to become operational in 1968, and the total program is to be completed by the year 2010 — in time to benefit your generation's children and grandchildren.

The nation's watershed plans have not all been centered in state and federal agencies. A number of programs have been initiated and organized by groups of lay citizens who, spurred by some major disaster, have roused themselves to action.

The date 1913 is remembered by the people of Ohio and Indiana as the year of the Great Flood. For days and days it "rained pitchforks and hay ladders." When the swollen waters of the Ohio River and its northern tributaries receded, five hundred lives had been taken, and the damage to property ran into the hundreds of millions.

In Dayton, Ohio, the bewilderment caused by this disaster quickly gave way to a determination to control floods. Citizens of the city, by voluntary subscription, raised a fund of more than two million dollars to study the problem of flood control. Their efforts led to the passage of the Ohio Conservancy Act of 1914, and the completion within a decade of flood-control works in the Miami River Valley.

Strict water control turned this unnavigable river (left) into a deep-water, all-year channel for heavily-laden barges (right).

This was the first time in this country that cities in a large river valley were fully protected from destructive floods.

Somewhat later, citizens of the Muskingum River Valley, in eastern Ohio, launched a great educational program, which after years of patient work, culminated in 1933 in the formation of the Muskingum Watershed Conservancy District.

Today, the eight-thousand-square-mile drainage area of the Muskingum River has been converted from a flood-ridden valley to a region of sparkling lakes, hardy young forests, rich productive farmland, and vast recreational wonderlands. As one resident put it "The people were determined to give their land a chance to amount to something." And the land has responded in full measure.

When the most recent of the great recurring floods struck the Ohio Valley in 1964, the gates of the Muskingum dams were closed at once. The operations of the flood-control reservoirs greatly reduced flood damage in the Muskingum Valley itself and contributed substantially to a reduction of flood waters on the Ohio River. Unfortunately, there is still a considerable portion of the great watershed

that has not been brought under control. If, instead of piecemeal solutions, a vast overall plan to control the interlocking rivers of the Mississippi, Missouri, and Ohio basin had been in effect, thirty thousand families would not have been made homeless along the Ohio. Nor would there have been an estimated hundred million dollars in property damage. Nevertheless, the Muskingum Watershed Conservancy District stands as an outstanding example of a citizens' program which, with the cooperation of state and federal agencies, has found at least a partial solution.

Throughout our country, hundreds of watershed associations, both large and small — watershed councils, soil conservation and conservancy districts, most of them private, non-profit, non-political organizations, are working to restore their land and water resources. We in the United States are not choosing any single way of doing the job; we are experimenting with a variety of methods. But the task has only begun. Of the eight thousand small watersheds in need of protection, only two thousand are expected to be properly cared for by 1970.

Despite the time it takes us to swing into action, and regardless of the administrative structure we finally adopt, we know that we must deal with our water problems within the framework of the water-shed. Only recently have we begun to think of another all-important resource — the air we breathe — not in terms of single, isolated portions of the atmosphere, but rather in terms of the "airshed." As with water, so with air; we must henceforth do our planning on a regional basis.

Let us take, as an illustration, the case of Wheeling, West Virginia, situated in a severely polluted area in the upper Ohio River Valley. In the early days, when explorers first followed the Ohio River westward and southward from what is now Pittsburgh, they must have found the valley a place of extraordinary beauty and loveliness. The trading posts that sprang up along the river soon grew into towns. Cheapness of water transportation, and nearness to West Virginia's coal fields were among the factors that drew the steel industry to the valley. Industry attracted workers, and towns grew to cities. Soon the entire valley was a close-packed jumble of factories, mills, and dwellings, all crowded together in the narrow strip between the steep hills that hemmed the valley.

As industries and cities grew, so also grew the pollution of the atmosphere. Wheeling's air was the most heavily polluted of all. Finally, the residents decided to make an intensive drive to clean the sewer above them. A new and strict air-pollution control ordinance was passed, and put into effect. In addition, a qualified air-pollution expert was hired, and funds set aside for a program of education, persuasion, and legal action. Some beneficent effects were noted: drivers no longer needed to keep their headlights on at eleven in the morning. But a survey revealed that despite all efforts, the city's air was still shockingly dirty. The air-pollution control's engineer explained why, "The sources of our present pollution aren't ours any longer, but the whole valley's. So long as steel plants, power plants, and many other private and public sources of pollution in neighboring communities all along the valley continue to emit pollutants by the hundreds of tons daily, nothing we can do within the city limits of Wheeling will really clean up the air."

Thus, it became evident that nothing short of concerted action on a regional scale could solve the problem. The eight counties stretching along the valley, the twenty municipalities, the two states, Ohio and West Virginia, all were needed to create a program that would treat the entire valley as an airshed — a single air-pollution unit.

In 1958, the Ohio Valley Air Pollution Control Council was officially formed. The Council is a voluntary agency with dues-paying industrial, association, and individual members. A number of city governments on either bank of the Ohio River participate in its activities. The Council has pressed for new state laws not only authorizing each city to control its own local pollution, but also calling for joint participation and regional action.

State laws and municipal ordinances with teeth in them are part of the answer, strict enforcement another part, education and persuasion still another. But action, of whatever sort, must be in terms of the region; this is the prime requisite for the well-being of the region's individual parts.

Airsheds and watersheds (with all that they encompass) constitute great natural regions, as we have seen, and we are finally beginning to treat them as such. There are other regions that are man-created. These are the vast built-up areas we have already examined in earlier chapters, the areas that reach out beyond our cities, giving rise to the terms *megalopolis, subtopia,* or *spread-city.* Whatever the name, each of these huge entities represents a region, which might be termed a *manshed.*

The history of planning for the manshed, or man-made region, is still in its early stages. Let us trace part of the story of a single great metropolitan region on the eastern seaboard, one that has followed the already familiar pattern of rapid growth and resultant spread.

In 1922, a group of concerned citizens organized a committee, under the sponsorship of the Russell Sage Foundation, to make a survey of the area around New York City. The committee's chief task was to develop a plan for the region, the New York-New Jersey-Connecticut area, consisting of the twenty-two counties and five hundred and fifty municipalities situated within a radius of fifty miles of Manhattan. The report, issued in 1929, was called "Regional Plan of New York and Its Environs."

The Plan recommended a system of regional transportation facilities including highways, parkways, railroads, airports, and river crossings.

Further suggestions included a pattern of urban development involving industry, commerce, ports, parks, and residences. The Plan offered standards for city building to be applied in zoning and planning laws, in the renewal of blighted areas, the advance of private developments, and public works programs. Finally, the Plan proposed principles for city and suburban growth based on human need rather than human greed.

In 1929, to promote and continuously develop the work started by the committee, the Regional Plan Association — a non-profit, non-partisan organization — came into being. Over the years, the Regional Plan Association has played a significant role in helping to develop and improve the New York Region's transportation system, its regional park system, and its standards of urban development. The Association has no official status, but its advice has never gone unheeded. Its constantly updated Plan has been a source of guidance to governmental agencies, private developers, and investors seeking a better, more liveable region.

One of the most important features of a good plan is that it be flexible, namely that it keep pace with changing times, changing technology, changing tastes of people. Without such flexibility, any plan, no matter how well conceived, deserves to gather dust.

Today's chief factor in plan modification has to do with projected population growth. In 1960, there were sixteen million people in the New York Metropolitan Region. By 1985, Regional Plan Association estimates there will probably be six million more, with an additional four million by the year 2000. This means approximately ten million more human beings in the region in the next forty years.

In view of the possible effects of such growth, the experts at Regional Plan Association have taken still another good, hard look at the region and the way in which it is moving — the exodus from the central city of those white families with children, who can afford to do so; the increasing concentration of Negro and Puerto Rican families in their place; the lengthening distance from city and suburb to useable open space. "Is this the way the people who live in the region want their region to go?" asked the officers of the Association. They were determined to find out, and they wanted direct answers from the people concerned.

In the spring of 1963, Regional Plan Association launched its "Goals for the Region Project," an imaginative and ingenious way of finding at least partial answers to their questions. More than six hundred study groups were formed in almost every community throughout the metropolitan area. Neighbors gathered at group leaders' homes on five evenings over a six-week period to view specially prepared television programs, to discuss the issues raised, and to fill out questionnaires. A weekly pamphlet sent to each participant gave additional background information as "homework" for the evenings ahead.

Some of the topics included were transportation, the size of residential lots, the location of industry, open space, urban renewal, and community beauty. In studying and discussing these problems, group members became aware that, if the present policies and trends that make for *spread-city* continue, the region's future form will give most of its residents neither the benefits of the city nor the pleasure of the countryside.

When the responses to the questionnaires of the more than fifty-six hundred participants had been tabulated and analyzed, several facts became clear. The great majority — mostly exurban middle-class residents — like suburban living but will support measures to keep the central cities healthy. They want their cars handy, but are almost unanimous in urging better public transportation. They like private homes on private lots, but are willing to invest substantial funds in public parks, and will accept metropolitan planning to keep the natural countryside from being completely swallowed up. Though, to the regret of its sponsors, the Goals for the Region Project did not represent a true cross-section of the population, and though the Project's findings were admittedly little more than straws in the wind, nevertheless the information obtained is helpful to the Association as it prepares new guidelines for the development of New York's Metropolitan Region.

Quite as important, however, for the future of the city and its environs is the direct influence of those who took part in the Project. While examining the direction in which the region was going, the discussants began to wonder whether present trends and policies *had* to continue, or whether they could possibly be redirected. It wasn't long before individuals and groups came to the conclusion that they themselves might take a hand in the shaping of things to come. A number of the men and women who participated are no doubt today speaking up on the issues they found important, and are seeing to it that their views are heard by the groups entrusted with the responsibility for making decisions.

Another association of people with influence on decision making in the New York area is the Metropolitan Regional Council, a voluntary association of elected municipal and county chief executives of New York and its bordering states of New Jersey and Connecticut. These officials meet regularly to consult on matters of mutual interest and concern.

On the action level, New York has combined forces with its neighbor, New Jersey, for certain specific purposes. Together, the two states guard the beautiful parklands on top of the Hudson River's bold cliffs through the agency of the New York-New Jersey Palisade Interstate Park Commission. Then there is the well-known Port of New York Authority, charged with responsibility for building and operating bridges, tunnels and airports for the bi-state area. As for other problems of "to and fro," a Tri-State Transportation Commission of New York, New Jersey and Connecticut is even now in the making. Along with the Federal Government, the Commission is to bring into being a Regional Transportation Compact. By the time you read these lines, both Commission and Compact may be realities — that is, if New Jersey joins the others in ratifying.

We have just examined rather closely one metropolitan area and its complex of organizations, both official and unofficial, each trying to bring order out of the chaos of the man-made region. We might equally well have selected some other metropolitan area on our continent — Toronto, Miami, Philadelphia, Cleveland, San Francisco, Chicago and others — each actively attempting to find solutions to the problems of its increasingly large and complex environment. Some of us shy away from "bigness" in governing bodies for fear that the individual be lost in the shuffle. Nevertheless, our nation was founded on the philosophy that there is strength in union; that it is possible through federation to band together for the larger tasks that can only be handled by joint effort; and that we can at the same time preserve what we value in local autonomy.

And we dare not stop with the region, for the region, whether natural or man-made, is part of a still larger whole — the nation. It is for this reason that some of our plans must be, and indeed have from the beginning been, national in scope. And each nation is piece of a still larger whole whose parts are inescapably linked together. To preserve this largest whole of all — our planet Earth — we know that we must begin to think in global terms.

But you and I — where do *we* make a start?

9 / Back to Our Town

To make a beginning, you must start where you are. This means you commence with Our Town and gradually reach out beyond it to the region, the nation, the world. At first, however, even Our Town is too large a whole. To cut it to starting size, you might better divide it into neighborhood, street, and home.

Immediately, you discover you are involved. Take this very morning, as an example. You walk through the kitchen and are dimly aware of a plopping sound. "That drip of an old faucet!" flashes through your mind. Suddenly you pause, for you remember there is a threatened water shortage in Our Town and in the other towns beyond. The papers have been full of it.

You stop long enough to put a large bowl under the faucet to catch the drops while you are away at school. You determine to conduct a small experiment. How much water will there be in the bowl when you return? How much would that add up to in twenty-four hours; in a month; in three months (the usual period of a water bill)? What does one leaky faucet cost the family? You resolve to repair that fixture without delay, and the one in the bathroom, too. But first you will need to learn how.

On another day, you are coming up the short path that leads to the front door of your house. You notice that the ground cover on the gentle slope is all scuffed or washed away and that gulleys are beginning to form. You decide to restore the damaged areas, but you will first need to know what is the most effective method of erosion control.

Now that you have become interested in land and the consequences of its careless use, you take a fresh look at the school grounds. The erosion is even more serious there than at home. "Could *we* take care of this?" you wonder. "We might even draw up a complete plan of land improvement and gradually put it into operation." When the thought is suggested in class, everyone is full of ideas and questions: "Let's beautify the school grounds by planting bulbs and shrubbery at appropriate places. What kinds of bushes would attract birds? We might set up demonstration plots to illustrate principles of correct and incorrect land use. What consultants and advisors ought we to seek?"

One thing leads to another. You and your classmates might one day find yourselves helping to rehabilitate the open spaces of your neighborhood or your town. The young people of Newton, Massachusetts took on just such responsibilities, when, during several recent summers, they restored to usefulness their town's neglected Edmand's Park.

Next, there is the evening when your father comes home with the rumor that a new factory is coming to town. He is enthusiastic, for he feels it will mean additional jobs for the townspeople and welcome tax money for the village treasury. Your mother worries about the location of the building — will the smoke from the new stacks blacken her curtains and ruin her plants? You ask, "Does Our Town

In Tiburon, California, teenagers and their parents gave their little town a new look in one weekend with donated paints.

have zoning ordinances to keep factories, businesses, and homes apart?" All agree that this is a crucial question, that it is important to know what ordinances there are, and whether they are adequate. If zoning regulations are nonexistent or if they are in need of revision, and if there are no smoke-control rules, it is high time, the family decides, for these matters to be considered at a town meeting.

Your parents do attend the next village board meeting and arrive home with some exciting news. An architect-planning firm has been hired to draw up a Master Plan for Our Town. You bring the report to class and find that others are interested, too, and want to follow the progress of the plan.

You learn that the first step will be the making of a *land-use* survey to determine the present use of each parcel of land in the community. You prick up your ears. You soon hear of other projects — an *origin-and-destination* survey to study the flow of traffic; an *opinion* survey, conducted by a local civic group, to determine what each resident wants most for his community. Perhaps the people doing all this research could use an extra hand — even an inexperienced one. There is enough part-time and summer work — if you are determined, and the adult "surveyors" willing — to obtain useful experience and gain a few important insights into the planning process.

Your mind jumps and you are suddenly thinking about your future courses at school. Physics sounds hard, but you'll need it to understand the basic laws of structure and architecture. Math, too. And that course in Mechanical Drawing would give you a needed skill. Knowing more about people, their customs and their needs, would be important. That's where social studies come in.

Your present year in Biology will help, too. You've already been busy learning something about the interrelationships of living things and their environment. You know that in the past too little attention was paid to these relations and that the consequences, in many cases, were disastrous.

All at once, you stop in your tracks. Think you could do it better, do you? Well, you'd like to try. It must be that you are *planning* to be a planner!

The discovery — it has been coming on you gradually — sends you back to the original sketch or model of an imaginary town you made when you started reading this book. How many alterations would you make in light of your present knowledge? Did you, for example, consider climate and geography and how these vital factors might affect your design? Did you provide adequate transportation both within and around the village borders? Did you leave enough space for expansion and did you also provide a belt of green as protection against urban sprawl?

You are, of course, well aware that there are still large gaps in your knowledge — a great number of things you need to learn before you are ready to produce adequate plans for even the smallest hamlet.

It will be important to re-examine your post-high school ideas, even if the time is still distant, and to find out what colleges or universities will give you the best training. There must be a number of such institutions. Post-graduate work will no doubt be indicated when the time comes. Perhaps there will be a period of apprenticeship with one of the world's great planners. You are certainly spinning dreams and running way ahead of yourself.

Next day, back to earth, you seek more concrete information from your school guidance counselor. She tells you there are over two dozen institutions — MIT, Georgia Tech, the Universities of Pennsylvania, North Carolina, Illinois, and California among them — each offering fine courses in the fields of city and regional planning. Some put special emphasis on urban design.

You inquire about the opportunities available once you have finished your training. You learn that the field is wide open. All over the country, towns and cities are awakening to the need for planning. Good planners are in demand in many units of government, from city and county planning commissions, to state planning and

High school students on a conservation field trip inspect large gullies in California and learn how to control them.

development agencies, departments of natural resources and public works, and on up to federal bureaus.

Planners, too, find employment in large industrial firms. Some planners act as consultants to government and industry in this country and in overseas nations as well. Consultants from the United States are especially active in Asia, Africa, and the Latin American countries.

Your counselor hands you an old news clipping. It tells the story of a group of thirty-four experts who met informally on a week-long cruise of the Aegean Sea during the summer of 1963. Called together by Constantinos Doxiadis, one of the world's busiest planners of new cities, these men and women from fifteen different nations and from such varying professions as economics, anthropology, sociology, planning, architecture, history, geography, and law, worked out a statement of principles known as the "Declaration of Delos." In it they suggested the establishment of a new discipline of *human settlements* to which other relevant disciplines would each contribute a share. They urged the initiation of far-reaching basic research, the working out of new methods of training leaders, and of attracting some of the best young minds into this new area of research, development, and practice.

You don't know about being one of the "best" young minds, but you do know you'll follow the parting advice of your counselor — to go home, do some reading, and take careful stock of your tastes, your talents, and your temperament in light of the demands to be made on you if you enter this field.

Planning, to start with, involves the art of design. But it involves much more. It presupposes a knowledge of the physical world the planner must alter; it assumes an understanding of the basic needs and aspirations of the people whom the planner must stand ready to serve. Put another way, the planner must have a working knowledge of many languages — the language of words, of aesthetics, of economics, of spacial, social, and ecological relationships. To become a molder of the environment, one who changes the face of the earth, is indeed a heavy responsibility and requires thorough preparation.

The field of planning may be approached through architecture and urban design, where plans are conceived, or through public administration, where plans are brought to fruition. To become a good planner, you must have mastery in one particular skill and an adequate acquaintance with many others.

As to temperament, you must first of all like people and be able to get along with many different kinds. You will not be working in a vacuum or running a one-man show. You will have to be willing to listen, and to cooperate with others whose specialties are concerned with the planning process. Essentially, your work will be one of coordinator of the many-faceted activities and the varied groups that are needed to make plans materialize.

You will need the ability to stand up to those who oppose planning because they do not like it on general principles, or because they refuse to acknowledge the need, or because they feel that their private interests may be in jeopardy. You must be able to compromise when compromise is sensible and necessary. At the same time, you must be ready to stand firm when you believe that to yield would spell nothing but disaster. Are you tactful? Are you patient? Are you willing to start over again when there is deadlock and frustration? And, above all, do you like to dream dreams?

The remarkable New Englander, Henry David Thoreau, wrote a book more than a century ago in which he described his own unique design for living. In the last pages of *Walden,* you will come upon these lines: "If you have built castles in the air, your work need not be lost; that is where they should be. Now put the foundations under them."

Education for the Planning Professions

Institution and Planning Program	Degrees Offered
UNIVERSITY OF CALIFORNIA Dept. of City & Regional Planning Berkeley 4, California	Master of City Planning
CASE INSTITUTE OF TECHNOLOGY Dept. of Civil Engineering University Circle, Cleveland 6, Ohio	M.A. in Planning
UNIVERSITY OF CINCINNATI College of Applied Arts, Cincinnati 21, Ohio	B.S. (major in City Planning)
COLUMBIA UNIVERSITY School of Architecture, New York 27, N.Y.	B.S. in Planning; M.S. in Planning & Housing; Ph.D
CORNELL UNIVERSITY Dept. of City and Regional Planning Ithaca, New York	Master of Regional Planning; Ph.D
GEORGIA INSTITUTE OF TECHNOLOGY Dept. of City and Regional Planning Atlanta, Georgia	Master of City Planning

Institution and Planning Program	*Degrees Offered*
HARVARD UNIVERSITY Dept. of City & Regional Planning Graduate School of Design, Robinson Hall Cambridge 38, Mass.	Master in City Planning; Master in Regional Planning; Ph.D
UNIVERSITY OF ILLINOIS Dept. of City Planning, Urbana, Illinois	B.S. in City Planning; M.S. in City Planning
ILLINOIS INSTITUTE OF TECHNOLOGY Dept. of Architecture and City Planning Chicago 16, Illinois	B.S. in City and Regional Planning; M.S. in City and Regional Planning; Ph.D
IOWA STATE COLLEGE Dept. of Landscape Architecture Ames, Iowa	B.S. in L.A. (Planning Option); M.S. (Town and Regional Planning major)
KANSAS STATE UNIVERSITY Div. of Engineering, Manhattan, Kansas	Master of Regional Planning
MASSACHUSETTS INSTITUTE OF TECHNOLOGY Dept. of City and Regional Planning Cambridge 39, Mass.	Master in City Planning; Ph.D
MIAMI UNIVERSITY Dept. of Architecture, Oxford, Ohio	Master in City Design
UNIVERSITY OF MICHIGAN College of Architecture and Design Ann Arbor, Mich.	B. Arch. (Planning Option); Master of City Planning
MICHIGAN STATE UNIVERSITY Dept. of Landscape Architecture and Urban Planning, East Lansing, Mich.	B.S. (major in Urban Planning); Master of Urban Planning
UNIVERSITY OF MISSISSIPPI Council of Urban Planning, University, Miss.	Master of City Planning
NEW YORK UNIVERSITY Graduate School of Public Administration 4 Washington Square, No., New York 3, N.Y.	Master of Public Administration
UNIVERSITY OF NORTH CAROLINA Dept. of City & Regional Planning Chapel Hill, N.C.	Master of Regional Planning; Ph.D
OHIO STATE UNIVERSITY School of Architecture, Columbus 10, Ohio	Master of City Planning

Institution and Planning Program	*Degrees Offered*
UNIVERSITY OF OKLAHOMA Institute of Community Development Norman, Oklahoma	Master of Regional and City Planning
UNIVERSITY OF OREGON Dept. of Landscape Architecture and Urban Planning, Eugene, Oregon	M.S. in Urban Planning; M.A. in Urban Planning
UNIVERSITY OF PENNSYLVANIA Dept. of City Planning, Philadelphia 4, Pa.	Master in City Planning; Ph.D
PRATT INSTITUTE OF TECHNOLOGY School of Architecture, Brooklyn, N.Y.	M.S. in Planning
RUTGERS UNIVERSITY College of Engineering New Brunswick, New Jersey	A.B., B.S. (Option in Planning)
UNIVERSITY OF SOUTHERN CALIFORNIA School of Public Administration Los Angeles 7, Calif.	M.S. in City and Regional Planning
UNIVERSITY OF TEXAS Inter-Departmental Committee on Planning Austin 12, Texas	M.S. in Community and Regional Planning
UNIVERSITY OF VIRGINIA School of Architecture, Charlottesville, Va.	Bachelor of City Planning
VIRGINIA POLYTECHNIC INSTITUTE Dept. of Architecture, Blacksburg, Virginia	M.S. in Urban and Regional Planning
UNIVERSITY OF WASHINGTON College of Architecture and Urban Planning Seattle 5, Washington	Bachelor of Urban Planning; Master of Urban Planning
WAYNE STATE UNIVERSITY Dept. of Urban Planning Detroit 2, Michigan	Master of Urban Planning
UNIVERSITY OF WISCONSIN Dept. of Political Science Madison 6, Wisconsin	B.S. (major in Regional Planning); M.A. and M.S. in Regional Planning
YALE UNIVERSITY Graduate Program in City Planning Dept. of Architecture, New Haven, Conn.	Master of City Planning

Institution and Planning Program	Degrees Offered
Canadian Schools	
UNIVERSITY OF BRITISH COLUMBIA Committee on Community and Regional Planning, Vancouver, B.C.	M.A. or M.Sc. in Planning
UNIVERSITY OF MANITOBA School of Architecture, Winnipeg, Man.	M.Arch.; M.Sc. in Community Planning
MCGILL UNIVERSITY Committee on Physical Planning School of Architecture, Montreal, Quebec	M.A.; M.Sc.
UNIVERSITY OF MONTREAL Institute of Planning, Montreal, Quebec	M.A. in Town Planning
UNIVERSITY OF TORONTO Division of Town and Regional Planning Toronto, Ontario	Diploma Course

Fellowships and Scholarships
There are three nation-wide fellowship and scholarship programs available in the fields of planning, urban renewal, redevelopment, and housing. They are: The Loula D. Lasker Fellowship Trust, Room 800, 917 — 15th Street, Washington, D.C. 20005; the Sears Roebuck Foundation, 3333 W. Arthington Street, Chicago 7, Illinois; and the Pittsburgh Plate Glass Foundation, One Gateway Center, Pittsburgh 22, Pennsylvania.

Grateful acknowledgement is made to the American Society of Planning Officials and the American Institute of Planners who jointly compiled the above list of colleges and universities.

Selected Reading List

The Environment

Clawson, Marion: *Land for Americans: Trends, Prospects, and Problems.* Chicago: Rand McNally & Co.; 1963.

Storer, John: *The Web of Life, a First Book on Ecology.* New York: The Devin-Adair Co.; 1953 (Paperback, Signet).

Udall, Stewart L.: *The Quiet Crisis.* New York: Holt, Rinehart and Winston; 1963.

A Place To Live. Yearbook of Agriculture. Washington, D.C.: U.S. Department of Agriculture; 1964.

The City

Editors of Fortune Magazine: *The Exploding Metropolis.* New York: Doubleday and Company, Inc.; 1958.

Elias, C. E. and others: *Metropolis — Values in Conflict.* Belmont, California: Wadsworth Publishing Co., Inc.; 1964.

Jacobs, Jane: *The Death and Life of Great American Cities.* New York: Random House, Inc.; 1961.

Mumford, Lewis: *The City in History: Its Origins, Its Transformations, and Its Prospects.* New York: Harcourt, Brace and World, Inc.; 1961.

Stein, Clarence S.: *Toward New Towns for America.* New York: Reinhold Publishing Corp.; 1957.

Tunnard, Christopher and Boris Pushkarev: *Man-Made America: Chaos or Control.* New Haven: Yale University Press; 1963.

Tunnard, Christopher and Henry Hope Reed: *American Skyline: The Growth and Form of Our Cities and Towns.* New York: The New American Library Mentor Book; 1956.

Water

Leopold, Luna B. and Walter B. Langbein: *Primer on Water.* Washington, D.C.: U.S. Geological Survey; 1960.

Water. Yearbook of Agriculture. Washington, D.C.: U.S. Department of Agriculture; 1955.

Clean Water — A Challenge to the Nation. Washington, D.C.: U.S. Public Health Service; 1960.

Air

Holly, Hazel: *What's in the Air?* New York: Public Affairs Pamphlet; 1958.

West, Wallace: *Clearing the Air, a Layman's Guide to Atmospheric Purity.* New York: American Petroleum Institute; 1961.

Open Space

Bolin, Luis: *National Parks of the United States.* New York: Alfred A. Knopf, Inc.; 1962.

Strong, Ann Louise: *Preserving Urban Open Space.* Washington, D.C.; Urban Renewal Administration; 1963.

Whyte, William H.: *Cluster Development.* New York: American Conservation Association; 1964.

The Race for Inner Space. Washington, D.C.: Department of the Interior, Office of the Secretary; 1964.

America's Wonderland. Washington, D.C.: National Geographic Society; 1959.

Transportation

Owen, Wilfred: *The Metropolitan Transportation Problem.* Washington, D.C.: The Brookings Institution; 1956.

Smith, Wilbur and Associates: *Future Highways and Urban Growth.* Detroit, Michigan: Automobile Manufacturers Association; 1961.
"Transportation and the City." *Architectural Forum.* Volume 118, no. 10; (October 1963), pp. 61-94.

The Region
Kerr, Robert S.: *Land, Wood, and Water.* New York: Fleet Publishing Corp.; 1960.
Lilienthal, David E.: *TVA — Democracy on the March.* New York: Harper and Row, Publishers; 1953.
Tunis, John R.: *Son of the Valley.* New York: William Morrow and Co., Inc.; 1949.
Goals for the Region. New York: Background Booklets, Regional Plan Association; 1963.
Valley With a Future. Knoxville, Tennessee: TVA; 1962.

Community Action
Abrahamson, Julia H.: *A Neighborhood Finds Itself.* New York: Harper and Row, Publishers; 1959.
Hubbard, Alice Harvey: *This Land of Ours, Community and Conservation Projects for Citizens.* New York: The Macmillan Company; 1960.
Smith, Herbert H.: *The Citizen's Guide to Planning.* West Trenton, New Jersey: Chandler-Davis; 1961.
ACTION Pamphlets. New York: American Council to Improve Our Neighborhoods, 2 West 46th Street.
Community Development Series. Washington, D.C.: Chamber of Commerce of the United States.
ABC's of Community Planning and other pamphlets. Chicago: Sears, Roebuck and Company.

Planning As A Career
Berger, Marjorie S.: *Opportunities in City Planning.* Bayside, New York: Vocational Manuals; 1961.
Munzer, Martha E.: *Unusual Careers.* New York: Alfred A. Knopf, Inc.; 1962.
Oppermann, Paul: *Should You Be A City and Regional Planner?* New York: New York Life Insurance Company; 1959.

Grateful acknowledgment is made for permission to use the following photographs:

Allegheny County Bureau of Air Pollution Control, photo by Associated Photographers, 84 bottom; photo by John R. Shrader, 84 top

Aluminum Company of America, 102 top; photos by Branco Photographers, 136, 137

American Forest Products Industries, 119

The Architects Collaborative Inc., photo by Ezra Stoller Associates, 110

Brazilian Government Trade Bureau, 31

Chicago Department of Urban Renewal, 56

Consolidated Edison Company of New York, Inc., 5

Fairchild Aerial Surveys, 14, 104, 120

Government of India Tourist Office, 28 bottom

Victor Gruen Associates, photos by Gordon Sommers, 50, 125

Houghton Real Estate, Mamaroneck, New York, 8

I. M. Pei, photo by Ezra Stoller Associates, 53

Los Angeles County Air Pollution Control District, 88

Robert Mentken, title page

The Milwaukee Community Development Corporation, photo by Fred R. Stanger, 21

Monkmeyer Press Photo Service, 23, 127; Campbell Hays, 12, 34, 100; Fritz Henle, 134; Phil Palmer, 163; Roy Pinney, 133

National Park Service, 114; photo by Jack E. Boucher, 113 bottom; photo by George A. Grant, 113 top

New Haven Redevelopment Agency, 48 top; photo by A. Burton Street, Historical Society, 46; photo by Ezra Stoller Associates, 48 bottom

Philadelphia City Planning Commission, photos by Lawrence Williams, 2, 37, 40, 42, 44

Public Health Service, Division of Environmental Engineering and Food Protection, 67

Reston, photo by Nelson B. Gilbert, Palindrome Corporation, 25

Soil Conservation Service, U.S.D.A., 64, 65, 76, 140, 165; photo by Billy Jones, 160

Steel Products News Bureau, 102

David Stemple, 58, 98

Tennessee Valley Authority (TVA), 72, 143, 148, 150, 152, 153

U.S. Department of Health, Education, and Welfare, Division of Air Pollution, 81, 92, 94, 123; photo by New York *Journal American*, 78; photo by Studebaker-Packard Corporation, 90

U.S. Department of Health, Education, and Welfare, Division of Water Supply and Pollution Control, photos from Virginia Fisheries Commission, 60, 62

Walker Manufacturing Company, photo by Karl K. Kerns, 86

Wide World Photos, 28 top

Cover photos
front, from left: Soil Conservation Service, U.S.D.A.; I. M. Pei, photo by Ezra Stoller Associates; Monkmeyer Press Photo Service

back, from left: Fairchild Aerial Survey; National Park Service, photo by Rodich; Monkmeyer Press Photo Service

Diagrams and maps by Jerome Kuhl

Index

About the Author

Martha E. Munzer was graduated from the Massachusetts Institute of Technology where she was one of the first women to enroll in the Electro-Chemical Engineering course. From 1930, until she resigned twenty-five years later to become associated with the Conservation Foundation, Mrs. Munzer taught chemistry at the Fieldston School in New York.

While at Fieldston, Mrs. Munzer was active in camp work. She was head counselor for the Ethical Culture Camp and served as a director for one of the associated Junior Work Camps, camps for high school students engaged in social service projects. In 1948, she shepherded two dozen high school students to France to a European work camp. In 1952, she organized a Science Work Camp where students carried on individual research projects.

As an Associate at the Conservation Foundation, Mrs. Munzer has prepared materials to help teachers integrate conservation concepts into their science teaching. She has also lectured widely.